From Darkness Into His Marvelous Light

Arlene Branham-Jackson
From Darkness into His Marvelous Light

Published by Spines
ISBN: 979-8-89569-934-8

From Darkness Into His Marvelous Light

ARLENE BRANHAM-JACKSON

Contents

Train up a child in the way he should go, and when he is old, he will not depart from it.

- Proverbs 22:6

About the Author

My grandmother raised me: As I stated, with the help of two of my aunts. I was brought up in Somerset, N.J. I am the second oldest of six siblings (four girls and two boys). I have a twin sister who is five minutes older than me.

I was raised in a God-fearing Christian home, and I attended church services on a daily basis. My grandmother told me about the consequences I would reap from living a sinful life and the benefits I would reap for living a life of holiness unto God. Even though I was taught all of this, I still made bad decisions that caused me to experience some hardships as a child and right up until adulthood.

As a child, I was always picked on and put down by my family members because I resembled my mother. Being picked on and put down caused me to be an unhappy, angry, and resentful child with very low self-esteem. I would retaliate the only way I knew how: by arguing and fighting with my siblings and cousins. Fighting with my family members caused me to receive a lot of beatings and to be put on punishment frequently. I didn't know what it was like to hear I love you or to receive hugs and kisses or words of encouragement.

My mother was usually high on alcohol, and I can remember the smell of marijuana while riding with my father. I would see my parents only from time to time. I longed for their love and affection.

Feeling unloved and as if nobody cared about me, I made a

choice to turn to the streets, where I indulged in a life of drugs that caused me to experience shame, as well as physical and mental abuse.

I knew that this was not the life that I desired to live, so I began seeking help from several indifferent drug rehabs, only to find that none of them could help me. Nothing I tried worked, so I decided to turn back to the one person that I was told as a child to trust in: God!

Being drawn by the Spirit of God and having the willingness to surrender my will and life to God, I am now filled with the Spirit of God, which helps me live a saved and holy life filled with joy, peace, and happiness. When I go through my trials, leaning on God helps me come out victoriously.

This book is dedicated to my Lord and Savior, Jesus Christ. In Him, I move, breathe, and have my being.
To my mother, Brenda Elaine Davis Branham, and my father, Elton Boot Jones, for allowing God to use them to bring me into this world. I do honor them!
To my two children, Aaron and Alicia Branham, for having patience when they were unable to have my undivided attention.
To my beloved grandmother, Eula Mae Branham, who taught me what I needed to know for this life's journey. She kept the faith, ran the race, and finished her course. May she rest in peace!
(January 15, 1914 February 13, 1985)

Foreword

My mother loved to drink alcohol and party. As a result, she was not able to raise her children. She gave all six of her children to her mother. My mother would come to my grandmother's house from time to time to visit her children, and sometimes she would bring us gifts. I didn't fault her for not being a mother to me because I loved her. As long as I saw her, when I did, I was happy.

I really dont know how my mother was as a child because I wasnt there. All I know is that, all my life, I have been picked on and put down by my family members because they said I looked and acted like her.

Except for my twin sister and me, each of my mother's children has different fathers. My sister and I didn't spend a lot of time with our father. We would only see him from time to time, and because of that, feelings of resentment toward him were in my heart.

When my father did come to see my sister and me, his visits wouldnt last very long, and after hed leave, it would be a long time before he would come back to see us again. Because of that, I acted as if I didnt love him to keep from feeling the hurt that came from wanting to be with him. Regardless of how my father was, I still loved and missed him.

As a child growing up without either parent being there to raise me, I can still declare, without hesitation, that I always longed for and loved them.

I will always love both of my parents very much because they are the ones God appointed to bring me into this world. With God's help, I developed a close, loving relationship with both of my parents that has, to this day, continued.

Despite my upbringing, I've come to the realization that sometimes a person will make bad decisions that will place them in situations that will be impossible to get out of. However, if we turn to the only true and wise God, who has all dominion and power in His hand, and surrender our will and our way over to Him, He will meet us in the very state that we're in and deliver us out of any situation. There's not a problem too hard that God can't solve. There's not a hole too deep He can't get us out of. When everything else fails, try Jesus. There's nothing too hard for Him.

Writing this book, *From Darkness into His Marvelous Light*, I've learned the true meaning of Proverbs 22:6: Train up a child in the way he should go, and when he is old, he will not depart from it. It tells how important it is for parents to raise their children in the fear of God. Even though some children may stray, the godly principles that are taught to them will stay with them and give them something to fall back on.

My prayer is that this book will increase the faith of those who believe. For those who are not believers, I pray this book will inspire you to come to know, trust, and claim Him as your personal Savior.

In the matchless name of Jesus Christ! Amen.

Vital Statistics

It took me three years to overcome feeling inadequate and fearful before I could begin writing this book. When I became discouraged, I would quit writing, but God would always send someone to remind me of what He had commissioned me to do. They would encourage me to continue putting my testimony in book form.

I tried looking to people to get the help I thought I needed. I felt that I needed someone to guide me along the way. I felt if I could find someone who was more educated than I was, I would be all right. I wasn't totally depending on God. I had to come to the realization that Jesus Christ is all I need to do whatever task He gives me to do. Jesus is the number one teacher. I also realized that God wasn't going to let anyone get His glory, not even me.

After I made up my mind to obey God and trust Him to give me the help I needed to put my testimony in book form, I had to deal with many attacks from the devil. The enemy would attack me so badly that I would have to stop writing, go into my secret closet, and seek the Lord to be delivered from spirits that came to hinder me and for strength to continue writing. I had to fight against the spirit of sickness, pain, depression, and laziness. It was a seven year battle but through it all I realized I can do all things through Christ who strengthens me.

I thank God for His loving kindness, His tender mercies, and for choosing me to be a witness for Him.

IF IT HAD NOT BEEN FOR THE LORD JESUS CHRIST WHERE WOULD I BE?

Train Up a Child in the Way They Should Go...

My grandmother was a Christian woman who loved and trusted in the Lord. She raised my brothers, my sisters, and me in the fear of God. We never heard curse words or swearing in the home. My grandmother never left us with strangers, and we were always taught to respect our elders. She would walk around the house praying, singing, and giving God the praise. I would even hear her praying in her room late at night and early in the morning. My grandmother had an organ and a piano in the living room that she would play until she sang herself happy in the Lord. She would always talk to us children about the Lord, and she made sure we went to church. My grandmother would even have church in her basement. She would get some chairs and have us children set them up in rows like a real church setting; then she would have each of us pray, sing, testify, and play our tambourines.

My grandmother would preach to me for hours at a time. One of her sermons I remember the most is about the bottomless pit. She always said that if I didnt live right when I died, I would go to hell, be thrown into the lake of fire, and I would burn forever and ever, and the fire would be unquenchable. Those sermons would scare me so badly that I would leave her presence with my mind made up to live right, but as soon as someone started picking on me, I would act up so badly that my grandmother would whip me and then preach to me again. I love my grandmother because it took a lot of patience and love to raise six other kids after she had finished taking care of her seven children. My grandmother never said she loved me or showed me any kind of affection by hugging or kissing me; I guess it was because she hadn't experienced it as a child herself. As long as I had a roof over my head, food on the table, and clothes on my back, that was her way of telling me that she loved me. As a child, I didnt realize that I was lacking anything because how can you miss something you never had?

My grandmother was very strict, and she wouldnt allow me to go many places other than church. There was a community center a block away from the house where neighborhood children would come together and do different activities. When I asked her if I could go, she would find things around the house for me to do. By the time I was done, it was almost time for the center to close. She didnt like letting us out of her sight.

I was in the sixth grade. The school I was attending planned a field trip to Stokes State Forest for a week. My grandmother did not want me to go, so I had to beg my aunt to talk her into letting me go. The week before the trip, she agreed to let me go. We couldn't afford to buy all the things I needed for the trip, so I borrowed a lot of things. I needed other items, but I couldn't get them, so I went without them.

The house had to be spic and span. We each had different weeks to do the dishes. We had to dry and put them away and make sure the cabinets, stove, refrigerator, and table were wiped off. Everything in the kitchen was white. We had to scrub the floors on our hands and knees. All this had to be done before we went to bed. If it wasn't done, my grandmother would beat us out of our sleep with a belt, broom, switch, or whatever she could get her hands on.

I'm grateful to my grandmother for teaching me how to clean because if she hadn't taught me how to clean, I wouldn't be as strict about cleanliness as I am today. I'm also thankful to her for telling me about the Lord because if she hadn't, I wouldn't have known whom to turn to when I got into trouble.

There are some things I didnt agree with that she did, but I believe in my heart that my grandmother did the best she could with what she had and knew. I believe she taught us the way she was taught.

I love my grandmother because if she hadn't taken all of my mother's children in, we probably would have been scattered all over the place, without a chance of knowing each other. It took a lot of love and patience to raise children that she didn't give birth to.

As a child growing up I was always picked on and put down all the time. I was a very unhappy, resentful, and angry child. I had very low self-esteem, which caused me to shy away from people, and I didnt have many friends.

My sisters and cousins would say things like, You're just like your mother. I hated it when they said that! It wasn't because I didn't love my mother; it was because they were talking down about my mother and me. When my sisters and cousins picked on me, I responded by fighting and calling them names. They would go tell my grandmother I hit them or said something bad to them; she would beat me and then send me to my room, sometimes without anything to eat. I don't think she intended for me to go to sleep without eating because she would put my plate in the oven for later. Before I went to bed, I would send someone downstairs to ask my grandmother if I could eat, and most of the time, I would eat at the dinner table alone.

I couldn't understand as a child why my grandmother didn't whip them for picking on me since they were the ones provoking me to do what I did. The vicious cycle went on all through my childhood. Now that I'm an adult, I believe my grandmother wanted me to learn that I didn't have to respond to everything someone said by arguing and fighting.

At the age of thirteen, I started to rebel against my grandmother because I wanted to do what I wanted to do. I also felt that we weren't getting enough clothing and things. My cousins, who were living in the same house, would get more stuff than my sisters and I. Seeing this happen made me jealous, and I wanted what they were getting. I didn't realize my grandmother was doing the best she could with what she had and with what she was receiving from social services.

I attended a Pentecostal church nearby, where the pastor of the church also taught me how to pray, fast, and dress holy. The women in the church weren't allowed to wear pants; we could only wear long dresses or skirts that had to come way past our knees. We had to come to church with a hat or a prayer cap on our heads. In this apostolic ministry, they believed it was a shame for a woman to pray with her head uncovered.

On Friday nights, we would have all-night prayer at the church. If the children fell asleep, the pastor would come to us, wake us up, and tell us to continue praying. We weren't allowed to go to the movies or parties. I loved going to church to praise the Lord, to sing, and to play the tambourine. It had become a part of me. After service, I would come home happy, singing and rejoicing while I prepared my late-night snack.

My sister and I decided that if we went to live with a lady who attended the same church as us, we would get more things. In those days, the board of social services gave people who weren't kin to the foster child more money to raise foster children than those who were related to them.

My sister and I began to complain to the pastor of the church about how unhappy we were living with my grandmother. The pastor talked to the lady at the church to see if she would take us in. She said, "Yes." A few days later, a caseworker came to our home to ask us if we wanted to go live with the lady from our church. I'll never forget the look on my grandmother's face when we said yes. I could see the hurt in her eyes, but because I was so stubborn I didn't change my mind, so my sister and I went to live with the lady from our church.

Living with the lady wasn't like we thought it was going to be. It was very boring because we didn't know many people in the neighborhood or in school. To keep myself busy, I would ramble through the lady's daughter's letters that she received from a guy she liked in Jamaica. Within a year's time, the lady's daughter and I ended up having a fight because I went into her room and read her mail.

One day, the lady's husband brought a woman he was cheating with near the house. He didn't want his family to see her, so he parked the car a block away with the lady sitting in his car. His daughter saw him get out of the car, and she also noticed his mistress sitting in the car. When he came into the house, the lady and her daughter jumped on him and beat him up as they cursed him out, using words they weren't accustomed to hearing. My sister and I couldn't believe the words that were coming out of their mouths. When my sister and I went to church, we told the pastors kids what happened and what words were used because we couldn't believe what they had done or said as Christians. The pastor's kids told their mother what we told them. Then, the pastor and the lady with whom we were staying called my sister and me into the office and told us we weren't telling the truth and that we shouldn't tell things that went on in the home. I was mad because I didn't like the idea that they were calling me a liar, so I said I didn't want to stay with her anymore. The pastor said if we left the lady's house, we couldn't come back to church. We didn't care, so we left the lady's house and went back to my grandmother's house, and I never went back to that church again.

I didn't go to church very much after that, only when my grandmother made me go. After a while, my grandmother stopped forcing me to go to church, so I stopped going. She said she did her job; now it was up to me to choose the right way, but she still preached to me when I went into the kitchen while she was cooking. Sometimes I would sneak out the back door to keep from running into her, but there were times when I would go into the kitchen knowing she was going to preach to me for about an hour. After she finished preaching I would leave with the intention of acting better, but I always ended up doing something wrong again.

Even though I stopped going to church, my grandmother still stood up for what she believed was right. I still couldn't go many places; I still had lots of chores, and I still received many beatings for fighting.

At the age of fourteen, my sisters and I decided we wanted to run away, so we did. We left home and walked around until it was dark. After walking around the block a couple of times, we ended up going right next door to our friend's house. Our friend's mother waited until we were asleep, then she called my grandmother and told her we were at her house. My grandmother told our friend's mother to send us home the next morning. When we got home in the morning, my grandmother didn't punish us right away; she waited until we went to bed that night, then she crept up the stairs and beat us right out of our sleep. She was good at doing that. We never ran away again, but I still didn't want to listen to my grandmother, and I was still determined to do what I wanted to do.

The Beginning of My Drug Use

My twin sister and I decided to skip school with her best friend. Her best friend took us to her boyfriend's apartment. When we got there, her boyfriend's roommate was the only one there. Both guys were 23 years old, and we were only fifteen at the time. While we were there, he gave us beer and marijuana as we sat and listened to music. This was the first time I had ever tried drinking beer and smoking marijuana. I didn't say much because I was very shy, and I had low self-esteem.

We stayed over at the guys' house until it was time for school to let out. When we left their house, we were so high that our eyes were almost closed as we staggered down the street toward my sister's girlfriend's house. We went to her house to wait until our high went down because we didn't want to go home while we were high.

My sister's friend's roommate liked me, but I didn't notice it because I was naïve and wasn't interested in men or boys at the time. A couple of days later, the guy who liked me told my sisters friend to tell me he liked me and wanted to see me again.

At first, I said no because I wasn't interested in him, and I was shy, but my sister and her friend talked me into going back to the guys apartment. The guy who liked me was the same guy who had the marijuana and my sister and her friend wanted me to go with them because they wanted him to give us marijuana for free.

The guy who liked me attended college at Minnesota State, and he needed money to pay for his college tuition so he could finish his last year. I found out later, after we started dating, that he was selling cocaine, heroin, and some pain pills that he got from his doctor to make money for his tuition. He tried to hide it from me, but he couldn't because I began hanging out at his house every day instead of going to school. I would see people coming in and out of his apartment, and I wanted to know why, so I asked him. At first, he didn't want to tell me, but I kept questioning him about it, so he finally let me in on what was going on. He let me know who was coming to buy what kind of drug, who sniffed, and who shot up.

I wasn't getting high off heroin and cocaine, so I looked at them like they were crazy, and I thought I was better than they were. However, I did enjoy the money my new boyfriend made from selling drugs to them because he would buy me things and take me places with it.

It wasn't long before he and I started snorting a couple of lines of cocaine together. After a while, the cocaine would make me feel so hyper that I didn't want to have sex, so my boyfriend suggested I try snorting heroin and cocaine mixed together. Doing heroin and cocaine together made me feel up one moment, then down the next, and I would feel very relaxed, as if I wanted to fall asleep.

The first time I snorted heroin, it made me so sick I felt like I was going to vomit my guts up. My boyfriend told me not to worry because once I got used to the heroin, I wouldn't get sick anymore, which turned out to be true. After using the drug about three or four times, I didn't get sick anymore.

My grandmother didn't like the idea of me skipping school and coming in the house late, so she told us she was going to report us to the Division of Youth and Family Services so they could find us a foster home to live in. My sister and I didn't want to stay in a foster home, so we decided we would rather go live with our mother, who lived in a motel room in Pemberton, NJ.

After being with our mother for several weeks, my sister and I realized our mother wasn't concerned about what we did or how we ate. She would leave us at the motel for hours at a time while she went to the bar to drink. The only thing she did for us was register us in school, even though we would skip school to hang out with army men and party. My sister would always try to get me to go out with different army men, but because I was still dating my boyfriend, I refused to. I would go to my boyfriend's house on weekends, or he would come to Pemberton if we wanted to be together. I would never cheat on him until one day he gave me a sexually transmitted disease. He tried to say I gave it to him, but I knew it had to come from him because I never cheated on him. When he realized I hadn't cheated on him, he finally admitted it was he who had cheated with a prostitute in New York. After that, I didn't trust him anymore.

My sister and I went to Mount Holly with this guy who knew our family. After we arrived there, the guy called the Division of Youth and Family Services behind our backs and reported us because he knew that we were minors who had been skipping school to hang out and party while our mother hung out in the bars, drinking and partying as well. The Division of Youth and Family Services sent a counselor out to get us to a juvenile center in Mount Holly, N.J. When the center called my mother at the bar to ask her if she had two daughters, she said no because she was so drunk she didn't care. I think it was hard for her to cope with the idea of my sister and me being with her because she was used to being alone.

My sister and I stayed in that juvenile detention center for three weeks and two days. On that third day, I told my sister, "I am running away.

My sister and I proceeded with our plan and pretended to take showers. We turned the water on and left it running so the others would think someone was in the shower; then we climbed down the fire escape outside the bathroom window. We ran all the way to a little mini-mall near my aunt's house. To our surprise, when we got there, my aunt was coming out of the store. We told her what we had done, so she told us to hurry up get in the car and put our heads down. She took us to her house for the night. The next day she took us back to our grandmother's house in Somerset, N.J.

That year, I moved back and forth from Somerset, NJ, with my grandmother to Fort Dix, NJ, with my mother several times. I even stayed in New Brunswick for a short time with my aunt. I was in and out of school. When I did attend school, I didn't have a clue what was going on. I wasn't learning a thing. All I wanted to do was hang out and get high, so I dropped out of public school altogether.

Finally, I stopped depending on my mother and grandmother for a place to live, so at the age of sixteen, I enrolled myself in a government program that paid me to go to school to get my G.E.D. and to learn clerical skills. I was on my own now, so I had to make sure I had a roof over my head and food to eat. I rented a room in a rooming house in New Brunswick. I knew that if I didn't go to school, my rent wouldn't get paid, so I went.

My ex-boyfriend's brother also rented a room in the same

rooming house where I lived. I would see a lot of people who used drugs going in and out of his room. If they came to his room, they had to give him some drugs first so they could use his room to get high in. Most of the women who came in and out were prostitutes. They would sell their bodies for sex to get money to get high. I would look down on them because I didn't have to sell my body on the street to get high.

My ex-boyfriend and I would use each other. On occasions, he would supply the drugs, and I would have sex with him. He wanted sex, and I wanted his drugs. I didn't think it was prostitution because we used to date. Even though I didn't see it as prostitution, it was, because if he didn't have any drugs to give me to make me feel numb, I wouldn't have sex with him.

I started getting high more than I went to school, so eventually, I decided to drop out of the government program. I needed to pay my rent, so I lied about my age and told the owner of the bar I was twenty-one, even though I was only seventeen. He hired me as a bartender.

I would steal money from the cash register at the bar where I worked to support my drug habit and to play my pick-its. I know the owner of the bar knew I was stealing, but he didn't say anything because he was an old, nasty man. After the bar closed, my boss would try to feel my behind and my breasts. To keep from dealing with him, I would ask my ex-boyfriend to be at the bar as soon as it closed so he wouldn't have time to try anything.

His wife caught him flirting with me a couple of times, so she decided to terminate my employment. After getting fired from the bar, I had to move out of the rooming house because I couldn't afford to pay my rent.

The Devil Tried to Kill Me

I moved in with my aunt, who let me stay in her house rent-free. To pay for my stay, I would try to keep the house clean, but it was hard living with eight children, all of whom were very young.

My aunt always took me in when I needed a place to stay. I'm very thankful to her for that. She never turned me away, and most of the time, I got along with her and the children, except for this one particular time when her oldest son and I got into a fight.

I was seventeen years old, and he was about fourteen; he was very strong for his age. My aunt wasn't home when he and I got into an argument over the children, and we started fighting. We tussled until he got me into a headlock. He had his arm wrapped around my neck, and he wouldn't let me go. The kids were yelling and screaming for him to get off me, but he wouldn't. They ran back and forth, in and out of the house, trying to find someone to get him off me.

The last thing I remember was hearing one of my cousins screaming at him, telling him he was going to kill me. The kids finally got someone who was passing by the house to come in and get him off of me. By the time the person got him off of me, I had urine and feces in my underwear. I didn't know where I was; I was dizzy and weak. It took me about five minutes to get myself together so I could go into the bathroom and clean myself up. I stayed in my room for a couple of days, trying to recuperate.

My cousin was the oldest in his family, so most of his siblings looked up to him. He was the one who had to watch over his siblings and protect them. He was the man of the house. I don't believe he meant to hurt me, and I don't hold it against him. He was only protecting his family, as he normally did. He was only trying to get them to do what they were supposed to do, but I opened my mouth and said something I guess he felt was sticking my nose where I had no business. My cousin was the kind of person who didn't like to argue, and he didn't like to be around confusion. When trouble arose, he would leave. My cousin has since passed away. He is loved and missed dearly. May he rest in peace!

I Held Out My Arm

I continued to bar hop and use drugs, and I started hanging out at the rooming house where my ex-boyfriend and his brother lived, and this is where I was introduced to the needle. Most of the people who came to my ex-boyfriend's brother's room used needles to get high. While I snorted, everyone else would shoot up. Those who used needles told me I was wasting the drug by snorting, so I let them talk me into shooting up. I was scared of the needle and the fact that this was an easier way to overdose but I did it anyway.

One day, I let my ex-boyfriend's brother shoot me up, and he hit me in my artery, and I couldn't move my arm for a week. I stopped letting other people shoot me up, and I would shoot myself up. I was so afraid I was going to take too many drugs and overdose, so I would shoot a little bit of cocaine mixed with heroin in my arm, then pull the needle out and flush the rest of the drugs down the toilet. My ex-boyfriend would get so mad at me.

One day, my ex-boyfriend and I took a trip to New York to buy some drugs. He took me to a shooting gallery. This is where lots of drug addicts go; they pay a fee to get high in the apartment. I saw all types of people there. I saw women shooting drugs down near their private parts, in their neck, leg, and anywhere they could find a vein. People would sit around, all doped up and nodding. If you didn't have your own needle, you could purchase a used needle from the people in charge of the shooting gallery. I was so scared of being there, I told my ex-boyfriend I wanted to leave.

We left and ended up going to Central Park in New York, and that's where we got high. When the police came and asked us what we were doing, we said nothing, but they didn't believe us; they knew we were high. The police officers patted my ex-boyfriend down, then looked around with their flashlights. They didn't find anything because when we saw them coming, we hid the drugs and threw the syringe away. They made us leave the park. After they left, we went back to get the drugs. We couldn't find the syringe because he threw it in the bushes. I told him, Lets go home, so we got on the next bus back to New Jersey.

Even though I was scared of the needle and the fact that I could overdose, I kept right on shooting up until one day I ran into this person who taught me how to smoke crack cocaine. When I tried it and liked it, that was just the right high for me because I could still get a powerful rush without shooting up. I felt that by smoking crack cocaine, I was less likely to overdose.

Smoking cocaine didn't last as long as snorting or shooting, so it took more to keep me high. Smoking cocaine was so powerful; people would get on the floor on their hands and knees, feeling around to see if they dropped some rocks or to see if they could find some cocaine that someone else dropped. That was crazy because we kept such a close eye on our cocaine that we couldn't have dropped anything. I would literally see people cry to get a hit of cocaine off the pipe. Even though I saw what the drug was doing to other people that didn't stop me from smoking crack cocaine.

When I first started smoking cocaine, I had too much pride to look on the floor for drugs, so when my cocaine was gone, I would wait around for other people to come to my ex-boyfriend's brother's room to give him drugs. He would give my boyfriend some, and then my ex-boyfriend would give me some. Or I would leave and go to the bar and wait around for someone who wanted to get high. If they didn't have a place to get high, I would take them to the rooming house.

Eventually, too many people started hanging around. After their drugs and money were gone, they would sit around and beg other people who came to the room to get high for some of their drugs. My ex-boyfriend and his brother got hip to what they were doing, so they started making people leave if they didn't have any money or drugs left.

Fewer people started coming to the house, so that meant we had fewer drugs to get high with. Eventually, my ex-boyfriend and his brother became really stingy with their drugs, so I stopped hanging out there as well.

I didn't want anything to do with my ex-boyfriend, but he was still in love with me, so he would harass me when he saw me at parties or at a bar, especially if he saw me with another male friend.

While I was at this after-hours club, he began to harass me. He tried to embarrass me by starting a fight with me. I left the club crying. Todd (who would later be the father of my son) pulled up in his car and asked me what was wrong. When I told him, he asked me if I wanted him to beat up my ex-boyfriend for me. I said yes, so he did. Todd beat my ex-boyfriend up and then put him in a headlock. I told Todd to get off him because I felt sorry for him. Todd let him up, then turned and looked at me like I was crazy. Then he left.

I had to call the police on my ex-boyfriend a few times until he finally realized I didn't want to be bothered with him anymore. I hated the very thought of sleeping with him because drugs had turned him into another person, and I didn't like that person. He was disgusting to me.

My relationship with my kids' fathers

I don't remember the first time Todd and I had a sexual relationship, but I remember going to his house often to see him. There were times when I couldn't wait until he came into the bar so we could leave and go have sex. Todd and I were never boyfriend and girlfriend; we remained friends even after he married and continued to have a sexual relationship.

I met Robert at a bar (who, in later years, would become my daughter's father). He was 50, and I was 20, but I liked the way he carried himself.

Lots of girls had their eyes on him, but I was determined to get him, and I did. I fell madly in love with him. He had everything in a man that I thought I wanted. He was a brick mason who owned his business. He also had money and a couple of nice cars. He was married but separated from his wife.

Robert and I had been dating for a year when he told me that he had another woman who lived down south. She decided she wanted to move to New Jersey with Robert, so he couldn't keep me from knowing about her any longer. Finding out that Robert had another woman hurt me very badly because I really loved him. I felt like my heart was broken into pieces. I continued to see him because he promised he would spend most of his free time with me, and he did. A lot of people didn't know Robert had another woman other than me, because when you saw him you saw me.

I hid the fact that I smoked crack cocaine from him for a long time. Robert thought that I just snorted a little cocaine and smoked a little marijuana every now and then.

When I felt like I wanted to smoke crack cocaine, I would hang out with him until he was ready to go home to his other woman; then I would smoke crack cocaine. Smoking crack made it easier for me to accept the fact that Robert was going home to another woman.

Sometimes Robert and I would go to the gambling joint so he could gamble. While he gambled, I would leave to go get high. When I didn't have enough money to buy any more cocaine, I would go back to the gambling house. I would drink some beer or liquor to come down off the cocaine high because I didn't want to sit there, paranoid, waiting for Robert to finish gambling.

I remember one particular time I had just finished getting high at my grandmother's house. My uncle asked me to throw his syringe away when I got outside. I put the syringe into my pocket; I was going to throw it away when I got outside, but I forgot.

Robert came to pick me up to go to the gambling house. After we arrived there, we got into an argument because I wanted him to take me to buy some cocaine, and he didn't want to. I started to get out of the car when he grabbed the arm of my jacket and wouldn't let it go, so I snatched my arms out of the jacket and got out of the car. When I got out of the car, Robert went through my jacket pockets and found the syringe. Boy, was he mad! After calming down, he asked me about it.

He thought the syringe was mine. I had to sit there and convince him that it wasn't mine. That's when I told him that I smoked a little cocaine every now and then.

"

Robert didn't like the fact that I smoked cocaine because he didn't like the way it made me act. I would get paranoid and start to hallucinate. While high off cocaine, I thought people were watching me from trees. I also thought people were out to get me. I would even look on the ground for cocaine because I thought I had dropped some when I didnt

Robert would get upset when I asked him to buy cocaine for me, but he would buy it for me anyway; sometimes he would just give me the money to buy the cocaine and then leave. I wasted thousands of his dollars on drugs.

Robert made sure I had money. Money was not a problem because he made lots of it. He would give me money for clothes and whatever I wanted. I believe he would have even bought me a car if I had had a license.

I started using cocaine more often because now I had nothing to hide. Besides, I was trying not to feel the hurt that came from knowing Robert had another woman. Using cocaine and because of the fact that I wanted Robert to be with me and only me, started to cause a lot of problems between Robert and me. He kept telling me to hold on but I got tired of hearing that so, I gave him an ultimatum. He had to make a decision if he wanted to be with her or me. He didn't want to leave her because she was sick, so I decided to leave him.

I got a job working at a hotel in Somerset, and I met an African guy. He and I began to date. He lived in a one-room apartment with his cousin and her husband. I, too, went to stay with them in the apartment. I don't think his cousin liked me, but she let me stay in her house anyway because of my boyfriend.

We put a twin-size mattress in the closet, and that's where we slept. Eventually, I was terminated from my job for missing days because of my drug addiction, and I ended up getting pregnant. After I became pregnant, I couldn't stand being around my African boyfriend. I couldn't stand the sight of him. I began to say and do mean things to him, so I decided to leave him and go back to my grandmother's house to live.

Back at my grandmother's home, I would often do and say things that weren't right and were very disrespectfulthings that, one day, would come back to haunt me.

I'll never forget this one dreadful thing I said about my grandmother behind her back. One day, I needed to use my grandmother's iron to press my clothes. She wouldn't let me use it because she was tired of other family members destroying her things and not replacing them. I got so mad I stomped up the stairs and said, "I wish she were dead! I didn't mean what I said because I loved my grandmother. I said what I said out of anger.

It wasn't long after that my grandmother became ill. I walked into her room and sat in one of her chairs. I wanted to tell her how sorry I was for saying what I said, but it just wouldn't come out. I couldn't bear to see her sick, so I jumped up and ran out of the room. It wasn't long after that my grandmother passed away.

For a long time, my conscience bothered me because of what I said about my grandmother. It wasn't until many years later, after giving my life to Christ, that I broke down in tears, weeping before God and asking Him to forgive me for saying I wished my grandmother were dead. God forgave me and lifted the guilt from my conscience. I understand now that I have to be careful about what I say and do to people because once it's said or done, I can ask for forgiveness, but I can't take back what I do or say. Proverbs 18:21 reads, "Death and life are in the power of the tongue and they that love it shall eat the fruit thereof."

After the death of my grandmother, everyone who lived in her house, except my aunt and a roomer, was out of control. We lost all respect for my grandmother's home. We started getting high and fighting each other in the house. The house that once was a place where prayers went up turned into a drug house. Any and everybody came in and out of the house. It was a wonder the police didn't raid the house and take us all to jail. I decided to move out of my grandmother's house and live with my two sisters. They had a two-bedroom apartment in New Brunswick, New Jersey.

I was five months pregnant when my ex-boyfriend came by my sister's house to see me. He had just come from New York, getting drugs. I asked him to give me some, but my twin sister told him not to because I was pregnant. I told him not to listen to her, to just give the drugs to me anyway, and he did. When he shot me up with the drugs, I didn't get high because the drugs went straight to the baby. Later that night, I began to have pains in my stomach. I lay there until about 5 o'clock in the morning after I couldn't take the pain anymore. I decided to go to the emergency room. When I got to the hospital, the nurses put me in a room by myself. In less than an hour, my baby girl came out stillborn. The nurse came in, took her away, then brought her back to me wrapped in a blanket and handed her to me so I could see her. She was the prettiest baby I had ever seen; she had a head full of hair and a light brown complexion. She had my complexion, but she looked just like her father. My baby died because of my drug use. I know the nurses and doctors knew it because they started mistreating me. I was so ashamed that I left the hospital without asking what they were going to do with her.

When I came home from the hospital, I told my baby's

father I had a miscarriage. He didn't believe me because he thought I had an abortion because I didn't like him and therefore didn't want his child. I never told him I used drugs and that's how my baby died. For years, what I had done to my baby haunted me, so I began to use more drugs.

Robert heard I had a miscarriage, so he came to the house to see me. He told me he was sorry I had a miscarriage. After my miscarriage, Robert and I started dating again, but it wasn't long before we began arguing about my drug use.

One day, Robert and I began arguing, and it became very serious to the point that we were ready to fight. Robert's sons tried to hold us back from each other, but I was so mad that I pushed his son, who was holding me away, so hard that he flew over the bed and landed on his bottom. Then I jumped between my sister and Robert's other son and cut Robert in the head with a kitchen knife. I just missed his vein on the left side of his head by his temple. Robert's sons had to rush him to the hospital. After I realized what I had done, I began to worry and pray, hoping I hadn't hurt him too badly. I walked all night, worrying about Robert, thinking about what I had done, and hoping he would be all right. I hurt the one person I loved and who I felt cared about me. My life was a mess and out of control, and I felt like I needed a change of scenery, so I decided to go back to live with my mother in Fort Dix.

While I was in Fort Dix, I met this guy I thought I liked who was a truck driver. He asked my mother if I could take a trip with him. She said yes, even though I hardly knew him. A trip that was supposed to be fun turned out to be miserable. We started arguing after we were thousands of miles out of the state of New Jersey. He got on my nerves so badly that I told him to drop me off at the next truck stop we came to. When we arrived at the truck stop, he announced over the CB that he had a "jersey queen" who needed a ride back to New Jersey. A guy responded and said he would take me back to New Jersey and told us where to meet him.

I got out of the truck that I was in and got into the other man's truck. He, I, and some other truck drivers, along with their women, sat in the truck at the stop that night, getting high while we watched prostitutes go from one truck to another. The other guy didn't want to leave me, so he came back to get me, but I wouldn't get back into his truck.

I rode in the truck with the guy from the truck stop for a month. We went from state to state, getting high and having sex. Sometimes we would have sex in the truck; other times we would get a hotel room. He treated me very nicely. I guess it was because we were having sex.

After we got back to New Jersey he told me if I wanted to come and live in Winston Salem, N.C. he would come back and pick me up even though he told me he had a woman in his hometown. Instead I went back to Somerset to live in my grandmother's house with a few other relatives. I ended up stealing my sister's jewelry and selling it for drugs. When she asked me did I do it, at first I said no, but then I turned around and told her I did do it. I was so embarrassed I ended up going to live in Mount Holly with my aunt. I felt that if I moved to Mount Holly I would stop getting high and that was also a good way to get away from Robert. After staying with my aunt for a while I called the truck driver and asked him could he come and get me because I was ready to live in Winston Salem, N.C.

He came to pick me up like he said. On the way to Winston-Salem, N.C., we took pills, smoked marijuana, and did cocaine. When we arrived in Winston-Salem, N.C., he had an apartment waiting for me. It was fully furnished, with food in the cupboard and refrigerator. He even got me a drug-addict roommate to help pay for the rent and bills.

I got a job at a hotel to pay my share of the bills. My roommate shot up drugs, and he talked me into shooting up again. He took me to the drug spot one time, and I remembered how to get there on my own. It was far, but I walked there anyway.

When my friend went on the road, I met these two guys who were friends of my roommate, and they also said they knew my truck driver friend. I invited them into the house, and we had a few drinks. Afterward, I saw them to the door.

They thought I was drunk, so they decided to break into my apartment after I fell asleep. When I woke up, it was pitch black, but I could feel one person lying in front of me and the other one lying behind me. They were going to try to rape me, but I woke up swinging like a wild animal, so they ran out of the house. That night, I was scared to death to go back to sleep.

My roommate worked nights. When he came home that morning, I told him what happened. He told me that the two guys who tried to rape me used to live in the apartment. They knew how to get in without a key or breaking the lock, so we boarded up all the windows.

When my truck driver friend came home, we told him what happened, so he changed the locks on my apartment doors and then went looking for the guys but never found them. A few days later, he left to go back on another truck run.

Robert wanted to get in touch with me, so he called my aunt to get my phone number. She then called me to see if I wanted him to have it. I told her to give it to him. Robert called me, and we made arrangements to meet up with each other in Wilmington, N.C. He said he would send me some money to take a plane there. After he sent the money, I spent all the money on drugs because I was still upset with him for not choosing me over his woman.

While my truck driver friend was on the road, I met another guy at an after-hours club. I ended up having sex with him because my truck driver friend wasn't around, and I wanted to have sex.

When he came back to town, he found out about it. It was a small town, and he knew just about everyone. He was mad about what I did, so he came to the house and started beating on me; I thought I was going to die. When he finally stopped beating on me, I told him I wanted to go back home. He told me when I first came to live in Winston-Salem, N.C., that if I didn't like living there, he would send me back home. He kept his word and purchased a ticket for me on the first bus back to Philadelphia. Robert and my aunt met me at the bus station and took me back to Somerset. Robert was so glad to see me. He explained to me the reason why he couldn't leave his other woman. He said if I just held on and waited, we would be together shortly. In my heart, I felt that Robert really loved me, so I continued to date him while he lived with his woman.

My Son Drugged at Birth

In the year 1988, Robert was home with his woman, and I wanted to be with him, so I tried calling his house and hanging up the phone to get him to come out to be with me. He wouldn't, so I went over to Todd's house to get him to come out and have sex with me. I knocked on his door and asked him to come with me to my room. I told him I wanted sex, but what I really wanted was companionship. While we were walking to my house, he told me I was crazy for coming to his house while his wife was home, but he also said he and his wife were having marital problems at the time and he was sleeping on the couch. At the time, I was living with another addict, a girlfriend of mine from whom I rented a room. Todd and I went to my room and had sex. This was the night my son was conceived. I moved back into my grandmother's house because I couldn't pay rent and my girlfriend wasn't about to let me stay there rent free because she used the money I gave her to support her drug habit..

I was pregnant and didnt know it. I got into a fight with

my brother. While we were fighting, he slammed me on the floor so hard that I had to go to the emergency room. The doctor ran several tests to make sure I was all right, and one of them was a pregnancy test. It came back positive; I was pregnant. However, I didn't find out until later because I left the hospital without being discharged, as they were taking too long, and I wanted to go home and finish getting high. I walked all the way home, and by the time I arrived, someone from the hospital had called and told one of my cousins to tell me I was pregnant. I needed to come back to the hospital for more tests to make sure the baby was all right, but I refused. I wasn't going to stop getting high just to go back to the hospital.

I felt as if I used more drugs while I was pregnant than I had in my whole life. Men would give me bundles of cocaine at a time, and I didn't have the sense to say no. I got very little sleep, and most of the time I wouldn't eat. I remember one day I didn't eat, and I figured if I took two vitamin pills, my son would at least get some kind of nutrition. I got so sick I vomited all the way home as I walked up the street. I walked a lot while I was pregnant. That was the only way I could get my drugs, unless I was with someone who had a car.

At first, I didn't know who my son's father was, but I had a feeling it wasn't Robert's because we were together for a long time, and I never got pregnant by him. Robert couldn't say much about my being pregnant because he had another woman, but we did stop seeing each other often because he didn't like the fact that I was pregnant and still using drugs.

I only saw Todd once in a while. I was going across the street to the corner store when I ran into him. He asked me if I was pregnant and if the baby was his. I told him yes, I was pregnant, but it wasn't his. I knew he felt the baby was his, and that's why he was asking me questions about my pregnancy. I told him I wasn't pregnant by him because I couldn't stand the sight of him at the time.

I started dating a Cuban guy while I was four months pregnant. He was a drug dealer and a drug addict, and he kept us supplied with drugs. We would smoke some of the cocaine, then sell the rest so we could go to New York to purchase more. After a while, we began smoking up all the drugs, so my boyfriend started selling baking soda as cocaine and ripping off big-time drug dealers to support my drug habit.

My Cuban boyfriend and I went to New York, and he introduced me to some big-time drug dealers. My boyfriend told them he knew a place in Mount Holly, NJ, where they could make lots of money. The drug dealers liked the fact that they would make lots of money, so they agreed to go there to sell some drugs. They said if I held the drugs while we drove there, they would give me some for myself, so I agreed to do it. My boyfriend and I drove in his car, and the drug dealers followed us in their own car.

On the way to Mount Holly, my boyfriend pulled over and asked the drug dealers if they didn't mind if we made a stop at my grandmother's house so I could run inside to take care of some business. When I went inside the house, my younger sister said she wanted to go with us, so I told her to come on. While I was in my grandmother's house, my boyfriend told the drug dealers he had to run across the street to the church to use the telephone to make sure business sales were up in Mount Holly, but he really went to call the cops to inform them that the drug dealers had drugs on them. I didn't find out what my boyfriend had done until the cops pulled the drug dealers over.

I was driving my boyfriend's car when I looked behind us and realized the cops had pulled the drug dealers over. My boyfriend didn't want the cops to notice him, so he sat slouched down in the car as I drove. I wanted to go back to see if they were all right, but my boyfriend told me to keep driving. We got away with all their drugs, and it was a lot about three ounces or more. After I put two and two together, I figured out what my boyfriend had done, why he wanted me to drive, and why he wanted my sister to ride in the front while he rode in the back. He knew that if two women rode together in the front, we wouldn't look as suspicious to the police.

We went to Mount Holly to my aunts house and got high until all the drugs were gone. While we were there, my boyfriend tried to leave me because he wanted to be with this other girl who had promised him sex for drugs. When I found out about his plan to meet with the other girl, we got into a fight. My boyfriend managed to wrestle me down to the floor and kept me there. My cousin jumped in because she didn't want him to hurt my baby or me. My family always sticks together when one of us gets into a fight. My other cousins were busy trying to find the cocaine pipe I threw at my boyfriend. Even after we fought, my Cuban boyfriend was still determined to leave, and I was still determined to stop him, so I burst out his side window with a brick as he was pulling away. He didn't want to ride around Mount Holly with no window, so he changed his mind about leaving. After all the drugs were gone, we had to drive back home without a car window.

When I was six months pregnant, I started feeling guilty about getting high while I was pregnant, so I tried to stop. I lasted two days without getting high. On the third day, I was in so much pain I cried like a baby. My son got in one spot and would not move. I thought my ribs were going to crack. The pain was so severe because my baby was an addict, and he needed the drug. He wasn't used to not having cocaine in his system, so my boyfriend had to go get me some. I took one hit of crack cocaine, and my son moved out of the spot he was in;

the pain left, and I went right to sleep. I never tried to quit using drugs again after that day.

My boyfriend and I started arguing a lot because he wasn't supporting my drug habit the way I wanted him to. One day, we got into another big fight because I wanted drugs really badly, and he wouldn't go get me any. We started arguing, so I went to sit on the front porch by myself. He thought I was outside talking to another guy, so he came outside to bother me. I cursed him out and slapped him as we went up the stairs. After we got upstairs, my mother, who was living in my grandmother's house too, decided that because I was wild and crazy, she would hold me back against the wall in a corner to keep me from hitting my boyfriend. While she was holding me, I realized he was swinging, but he wasn't hitting me, so I touched my face. When I looked at my hands, blood covered them. I realized he was cutting my face with a dull razor blade we used to chop up cocaine with. I pushed my mother out of the way and went running after him. He got away. I had to be rushed to the emergency room that night. I received stitches in three different places on my face: my right eye, my left cheek, and my chin were cut. It had been a while since I had a tetanus shot, so the doctor requested that I get one. The doctor said if the razor blade had been a new one, I would have been messed up for life.

My boyfriend was charged with assault with a deadly weapon on a pregnant woman. He didn't want the police to catch him, so he went into hiding. He wanted me to drop the charges, so he tried to win me over by sending me flowers through one of his friends. Little did he know that even if I did want to drop the charges, I couldn't because the state picked up my case, and they were the ones who had filed charges against him. I saw him in the streets a couple of times after everything had died down. Not long after that he moved to

New York City where he was stabbed to death for ripping off a big time drug dealer.

Robert and I started seeing each other again, and I didn't have any decent clothes to wear while I was pregnant, so he took me to the store to buy me something to wear. When I got to the store, I tried on size 11/12 pants, and they were too big. Then I tried on a 9/10, and that size was too big, so I tried on a 7/8, but they were too big as well. When I picked up a size 5/6, Robert gave me a hundred-dollar bill and walked out of the store because he couldn't believe how skinny I was.

I kept getting high right up until it was time for me to give birth to my son. He was born on January 26, 1989. I don't remember how I got to the hospital, the labor pains, nor the moment he came out. I used so many drugs during my pregnancy that it caused me not to remember my son's delivery. I do remember the doctor putting a tube or something inside me and attaching it to my son's head so they could monitor his heart rate while he was being delivered. The condition of my son after his birth wasn't a pretty sight. He had tubes on his head, arms, and in his feet. He had to be put in an incubator under a light because he was only 4 pounds. I felt so ashamed for what I had done to my son. It was because of my drug addiction that my son had to go through what he was going

Through. He had to stay in the hospital for 3½ weeks, and that still didn't stop me from using drugs.

The social worker at the hospital called the Division of Youth and Family Services because I didn't have medical insurance and my son was a crack baby. The social service worker sent a worker to the hospital because they wanted to know where I would be living, and they wanted to make sure my son had everything he needed. Even though I didn't have anything for my son, I told her I did because I didn't want her to take my son and I told her I would be staying with my mother and aunt in my grandmother's house.

My cousin and I went to the hospital to see my son. She said, Woo, Arlene, he is so cute! I'm going to the store and buy him something." We left the hospital and went to "Toys R Us." I thought she was just going to buy him a couple of sets, but God laid it on her heart to buy my son everything he needed. She brought him a bassinet, lots of clothes, bottles, t-shirts, a bottle washer, and some milk. She brought everything except for diapers. The only reason she didn't buy him Pampers was that his godmother had already brought him a box of 300 Pampers. I was grateful to my cousin for buying my son all the things he needed because the Division of Youth and Family Services would have taken my son away from me and put him in foster care if she hadn't done what she did.

My mother jokingly told Robert that he was my son's father. Robert knew he wasn't the father, but he wanted to make sure, so he and a friend of ours came by the house to see my son and me. While they were there, Robert gave me a hundred dollars to buy something for my son, but as soon as I came home from the hospital, I slipped on a pair of pants over my pajamas. Then my cousin and I went across the street to buy some crack cocaine. I bought ten vials of cocaine at ten dollars per vial.

When I was across the street, this girl started yelling at me. She was jealous because she couldn't buy any drugs. I told her to leave me alone because my body was still sore from just giving birth, and I didn't want to fight her, but she wouldn't, so I told my cousin to hold my drugs, and we fought. I beat her up, and she still wouldn't leave me alone because she was convinced she could whip me. We fought until my top pants ripped. I stopped fighting, took off my top pants, and went back to fighting her in my pajama bottoms. She thought she was the best fighter around, so she wouldn't accept the fact that she had met her match. She just wouldn't leave me alone; she followed my cousin and me all the way home. As she stood in the front lawn I told her to stay right where she was and that I would be right back. I ran in the house, got a big kitchen knife and chased her back across the street. Months later I ran into her again and she still thought she could beat me. We ended up fighting again and I beat her again. After that she found out she really couldn't beat me so she left me alone.

Before the social worker would allow the hospital to release my son, she had to come to my grandmother's house to make sure I had everything I needed for him. When the caseworker came, I showed her where he would be sleeping and everything I had for him. She was amazed at how much stuff I had. Her comment was, "He has more stuff than I do, and I have been living longer than he has." She told me to go to the hospital, pick my son up, and she would meet me back at the house to finish the rest of the paperwork. When I went to pick up my son, the staff at the hospital would not release him to me, so I went off! I started cursing at the nurses and threatening them. The nurses called the hospital security guard. The security guards came and pushed me down on the floor, handcuffed me, then took me to their office. I told them I wanted to make a phone call. I called my cousin and told him what was going on. When I looked around, half of my family was at the hospital fussing with them. They gave me my son because they knew they were wrong for trying to keep me from taking him home, and they didn't want any more trouble. They asked me if I wanted them to take baby pictures of him. I was so mad I told them what they could do with their hospital and their pictures and we left.

After my son was born, I continued to get high, but now I had to worry about who would watch him while I got high.

Sometimes I would ask my aunt or my cousin if they could watch my son for a couple of minutes while I ran across the street to the store. I never came back at the time I said I would. I would leave him with them for hours at a time. Other times I would make sure he was asleep then run across the street to get my drugs, come back and get high in the bathroom or in another room away from my son, but I would run back and forth to check on him.

Before I started getting high I would make sure my son was bathed and fed. I would sterilize his bottles and nipples, fill up about twenty bottles with formula and put them in the refrigerator so I did not have to make bottles when my son got hungry. Most of the time I washed his clothes out by hand in the kitchen sink because I would use all my money on drugs and I didn't have money to go to the laundry mat. The only time my son got new clothes was when my cousin brought them for him when he was first born and when other people gave him some.

I abused my son in many ways. I never showed him love and affection the way a mother should. I spent most of my time getting high or sleeping off my high. When I couldn't get high, I would get very angry and take it out on my son by yelling at him.

One night, Robert stayed the night with me. The next morning, when he got ready to leave, I told him I needed money to get my son some milk, but I really wanted the money to get high with. He put twenty dollars on my night table, then I fell back to sleep after he left. When I woke up I realized someone had come into my room while I was asleep and taken the twenty dollars. I was so mad I went through the house fussing and cursing like I didn't have any sense. I had formula to feed my son, but I wouldn't give it to him right away. I figured if I let him cry, someone would feel sorry for him and give me money so I could buy some drugs, but no one paid us any mind, so I finally felt bad and made him a bottle.

My drug use didn't lessen; it only got worse. After getting high, I would become paranoid and begin to do strange things. If my son had on a bib, the drugs had me thinking he was choking. I would pull the bib off him, then feel his chest to make sure he was still breathing. In reality, he was just fine, but after taking a hit of cocaine, you couldn't tell me that.

I need help! I'll try rehab

My drug addiction continued to get worse, and I knew I needed help, so I told my social worker I wanted to go to rehab. She found a temporary foster home for my son and a rehab facility for me. I couldn't ask any of my family members to watch my son because everyone was doing their own thing, and the majority of them were on drugs, too. My son was placed in a foster home in Somerset. Before I left for rehab, I met the foster family. They were a very nice family, and they fell in love with my son instantly. I knew my son was in good hands because the family had custody of three grandsons whom they took very good care of.

While I was in rehab, we had group meetings. One person had to sit in the middle of a circle surrounded by other peers. The peers job was to ask questions and try to get the person in the middle to be honest about what was hurting them on the inside. When it was my turn to sit in the middle, I said to myself, "They aren't going to make me cry," but as soon as they started asking questions about my childhood and my mother, I broke down and cried like a baby. In the past, whenever I would break down and cry, I would always make sure I was alone. This was the first time I let someone see me cry. After a week or so of being in the rehab facility, I was ready to go home because I was homesick and wanted to get high. I wasn't ready to stop using drugs; I just went through the motions until my thirty days were up.

A month later, in July of 1990, after completing my drug rehabilitation, I came home from rehab. I continued to use drugs, so my social worker suggested I sign myself into an outpatient rehab drug program. The outpatient program was a joke to me. I continued to use drugs while I attended the program; I lied to my counselor about everything, I didn't take part in any of the group discussions, and eventually the rehab started taking random urine tests. Of course, I always failed the test. The division of youth and family services threatened to take custody of my son so I had to go back into the same in-patient program I had just gotten out of a couple of months prior.

While I was in the in-patient program, the doctors told me they were going to give me an HIV test. I told them I didn't care because there wasn't anything wrong with me. After the test came back, the doctors called me into their office to give me my results. To my surprise, the test came back positive. I was in total shock. I ran to my room, closed my door, locked it, and I wouldn't come out. I was scared and ashamed. The only thing that ran through my mind was that I was going to die. The counselor came to my room and took me back to the doctor's office so he could talk to me. The doctor said just because I was HIV positive didn't mean I was going to die. He said, "Being HIV wasn't AIDS it was just the virus that causes AIDS, and if you stop using drugs and take care of yourself, you don't have to die from it". I was so upset that I didn't pay him any mind. The only thing I kept thinking about was that there was no cure for the AIDS virus and that it kills.

I was released to come home after being in rehab for thirty days. I told my son's foster parent that I was HIV positive. She knew a little about the disease because her daughter had died because of it, so she didn't treat me any differently. I must have contracted the virus after I had my son because he was tested, and his test came back negative. I told my daughter's father and my son's father that I was HIV positive. Knowing this didn't stop them from having sex with me without a condom. Their response was, "They had sex with me in the past while I was infected, so whatever happens, let it happen." After I found out I was HIV positive I began to use more drugs because I just didn't want to think about it.

I made a decision that it would be best for my son and me if I didn't go back to live with my aunt in my grandmother's house because of all the drug use that went on there. My son's foster parent agreed to rent me a room in her home. I hated staying there because she was so nosy. She would go into my room and look through my things when I wasn't home, so I put a lock on my door. She told me she didn't want any locks on her doors, so I had to take it off. Sometimes I would ask her to watch my son, even though I didn't like her watching him because I couldn't stay out as long as I wanted to without her saying something. I started staying away from her house more and more because I felt uncomfortable, and I didn't want her to know I was still getting high. I would put my son in his carriage and head up to my grandmother's house, where my aunt lived. When I arrived there, I would ask my aunt or my cousin to watch him; I would put him on one of their beds and take off to get high. They would watch him all day.

Eventually, I got tired of living with my son's foster parent, so I moved into a shelter in Somerville. I had to abide by a lot of rules. I had to put a certain amount of money in the bank from my welfare check, provide my own food, do weekly chores, and I had to be in by 9:30 during the week. If I wanted to stay out for the weekend, I had to get a weekend pass and undergo random drug tests. These rules didn't stop me from getting high. As soon as I moved into the shelter, I found out my son's father's wife was also living in the shelter. The counselors at the shelter thought we were going to get into a fight, but instead, we became the best of friends. We started hanging out at the park together. It wasn't long before we started using drugs together, and if one of us messed up we would cover for one another. I started messing up so badly that the counselors at the shelter told me I had to leave. I didn't have any money to get my own place because I spent it all on drugs, so the Department of Social Services put my son and me up in a motel room. I began to use more drugs because now I didn't have anyone to monitor me, and I still didn't have to pay rent. I would take my son with me to buy my drugs because I didn't have anyone to watch him. My round-trip cab fare would cost twenty dollars from Somerville to New Brunswick and back. I did this until the board of social services got tired of paying for my motel room. I didn't save any money. I couldn't get my own place, so I had to move back into my grandmother's house with my aunt, and I continued to get high.

Not long after, Robert's girlfriend passed away, so I started hanging out at his apartment. Eventually, I moved all of my things into his apartment. While Robert was at work, I made sure the house was clean, and I loved doing the laundry because Robert and his son would always forget and leave either a ten, a twenty, or sometimes even a fifty-dollar bill in their pants pockets. As soon as I found the money, I would stop doing what I was doing and head straight for the drug dealer to buy crack cocaine. Before it was time for Robert to come home I would drink some liquor so I could come down off my high because I didn't want him to know I had been getting high.

Robert's ex-girlfriend's things were left in the apartment, and every day I would take something from the apartment and sell it to get high. My mother moved back to Somerset, NJ, from Nebraska. She and I got a carriage that belonged to a grocery store. We took everything from Robert's apartment that we thought would sell. We put it in the carriage and walked around the apartment complex, going from door to door until all the items were sold. Then we used the money to buy drugs. Robert didn't notice the items were missing because he didn't know what his ex-girlfriend had in the apartment.

My Daughter's Conception and Birth

I always wanted a child by Robert because I loved him, and I wanted something that was a part of him. So each time we had sex, I hoped to get pregnant by him, even though I knew I was HIV-positive.

In November of 1998, Robert and I had company over to his apartment. They decided they wanted to spend the night, so Robert and I let them take our bedroom, and we slept in the empty room on the floor. That is where my daughter was conceived. A few weeks later, I started getting morning sickness.

During my pregnancy, Robert's younger son and I couldn't stand each other. We argued like cats and dogs. One day, Robert's son left his gold jewelry on the kitchen table. When I noticed it, I took it and sold it. He was so mad we almost got into a fight. Robert told his son not to bother me and promised him he would give him back the money for his jewelry. One night I slept with a big kitchen knife under my pillow because I was scared Robert's son was going to try to jump on me because we were feuding so bad.

Like usual, I wanted money for drugs, and Robert wouldn't give me any. He didn't want me doing drugs, especially while I was carrying his child. I got so mad at him. I took some rubbing alcohol, poured it on the living room floor, lit a match, and threw it on the floor. Robert and I sat there and watched the fire burn the floor. He said he didn't care, that I could burn down the whole house if I wanted to. The flames began to get high, and I realized he wasn't going to put the fire out. I became frightened, stomped out the fire, and left the house to try to find some drugs.

Another day, Robert and I got into a big argument over drugs and money. The situation began to get out of hand, so Robert called the cops on me. When the cops arrived at the apartment, I was crying. I lied and told them Robert had hit me. The cops tackled Robert to the ground, and while they were trying to put handcuffs on him, I started screaming, telling them to get off him. They let him up, and I decided not to stay at the house that night because I knew I was to blame for the whole situation. My son was staying over at my twin sister's house, so I went there to spend the night. I wasn't getting along with Robert or his son, so we felt it was best if I moved out of the apartment and back into my grandmother's house with my aunt. The house was out of control because everyone who lived there was on drugs except for my aunt and a lady who rented a room from her.

My aunt and her daughter decided to move out into their own house because Grandmother's house was going downhill. Neither the mortgage nor the electric bill had been paid, and no one would contribute any money for its upkeep. Finally, the lights were cut off, so we had to use candles to see. There was no heat, so we used kerosene heaters to keep warm.

My uncle started acting weird after my grandmother passed away because he took her death really hard. I was about 51/2 months pregnant at the time. We were in the house one day with no lights after the electricity had been cut off. All of a sudden, he came downstairs and out of nowhere, hit me in my head with a thick wooden stick that came off the organ stool. When he hit me, my whole body vibrated and I was dazed for a couple of minutes. The guy I was getting high with asked my uncle why he hit me in my head like, that saying that he could have hurt the baby and me. He just ignored us and walked away. I could no longer stay in my grandmother's house because it was unsafe for the baby and me. I moved into a rooming house where my twin sister was staying. This house was a little better. The lights and heat were working, but the septic tank was broken so we couldn't use the bathroom. We had to go to the bathroom in a bucket then take the bucket outside and empty it. It was disgusting!

I couldn't move back in with Robert because he let his stepdaughter move in, and she and I couldn't stand one another; she didn't like the fact that Robert and I dated while he was living with her mother.

Even though Robert and I didn't see eye to eye about my drug addiction, we continued to see each other. He would come to visit me at the rooming house where I lived. He still didn't like buying me drugs while I was carrying his child, but I would put up such a fuss that he would buy the drugs for me anyway. Then he would leave because he didn't want to be with me while I was high.

I started going to Robert's apartment, and if he didn't come to the door, I would burst out his car window. I went to his house one day because I wanted money for drugs, and he wasn't home. He had gone fishing, but I thought he was in the house because his car was parked outside, so I burst out the front window of his car. When I found out he wasn't there, I felt so stupid. Robert got tired of me arguing, fighting, and bursting out his car windows, so he packed his things and moved back down south. I didn't think he would leave me while I was pregnant, but he did.

The money my twin sister and I gave to my cousin for rent was supposed to go toward the mortgage on the house; instead, the money was going into his pocket. My cousin got an eviction notice, but he hid it from us. While we were still living in the house, the township came, put padlocks on the doors, and boarded up the windows with all our belongings locked inside. My twin sister and I needed our clothing and other items, so we went back to the house after it was dark, took what we could and the rest of our belongings we left there.

My grandmother's house was in no shape for people to live in, so I went to the board of social services to get help with a place to live. That night, they put my son and me up in a sleazy motel room on Route 1 in South Brunswick. I hated the motel because it was dirty, the bed was uncomfortable, I had to eat out every day, and I had no place to store my son's bottles. I stayed there for two weeks. Then I was moved into an efficiency apartment at a hotel in New Brunswick. I liked this room better because it had a kitchen with a stove, refrigerator, microwave, cooking utensils, a full-size bed, and I had my own bathroom. It was almost as if I had my own mini apartment, and it didn't cost me a dime. The only thing I had to do was wash my clothes and buy my own food. I received food stamps for food, and I could wash my clothes for maybe forty dollars a month. Another thing I liked about living there was that the drug spot was within walking distance, and I could get high with no one to bother me. I even made sure my son wasn't there. I would either take him to my twin sister or to my aunt and my cousin. Every chance I could get rid of him, I did. Even though I continued to get high while I was pregnant, I did try to cut back a little because I didn't want this child to go through what my son went through when he was born.

On July 1, 1990, as I began to cook chicken, my contractions started. After I seasoned the chicken, a contraction came; I put the chicken down and lay on the bed until the contraction stopped. I floured the chicken, and another contraction came, so I went back and lay on the bed again until the contractions passed. After I began frying the chicken, at least three more contractions came, and by the time I was done cooking all the chicken, it was time to go to the hospital because the contractions were coming too close together. I told my brother to call the ambulance because it was time for me to go to the hospital. When the ambulance came, I insisted they take me to a different hospital from the one where I had my son because I didn't want them to give me any trouble, like they did when he was born.

My brother watched my son for me while I was in the hospital giving birth to my daughter. He took very good care of my son, and he even brought him to the hospital to see me.

It wasn't long after I arrived at the hospital that I gave birth to my daughter. She was 5lbs 3ozs. The only sign of drug addiction was my daughter's leg would tremble from time to time. The next day after I had given birth to her, the doctor came into my room to tell me my daughter was HIV positive. The news surprised me and I was scared my baby would die because of the virus. Even though I was in denial of being infected with the virus, reality begun to set in once again. I felt not only was I going to die, but my daughter was too. I asked the doctor what were my daughter's chances of making it? She said many children don't make it past the age of 10-13 years of age after being born with the virus. She even said many children die as infants. The doctor told me the only chance my daughter had was if she developed her own blood and if the virus didn't carry over to her blood. The doctor said all we could do was pray and to wait. I didn't tell anyone what was going on with my daughter because I didn't want anybody to know I was HIV positive. The only people who knew I was HIV positive were my daughter's father and my son's father. I didn't have anybody to talk about what I was going through because Robert was in North Carolina and my son's father wasn't anywhere around at the time.

Even though the hospital staff and the social worker knew my daughter had drugs in her system, they didn't give me a problem about taking her home from the hospital. I had a place to live at the hotel. Also, she was born on the same day I received my welfare check, so I had money to buy her what she needed.

Having another baby didn't stop me from using drugs. As soon as I came home from the hospital, I wanted to get high. I had my welfare check, and the drug spot was right around the corner, so there wasn't anything stopping me from getting high. My brother watched my baby while I went to get the drugs; he was good with kids and overprotective of them, even when he got high. We didn't use the drugs in the same room where my daughter was because we didn't want her to wake up or catch a contact high, so we went into the bathroom. After every hit, I would run out of the bathroom to check and see if there was something wrong with her. Even though there wasn't, the drugs made me think there was something wrong. My brother would yell at me to stay in the bathroom and leave the baby alone because nothing was wrong with her, but I wouldn't listen. I thought she might be choking, or maybe she had stopped breathing or something. Sometimes I would even think people were standing outside my hotel room trying to listen to what was going on inside. I would get down on the floor to see if I could see someone's feet underneath the door. I would also stand as quietly as I could to see if I could hear someone outside the door. The least little sound would make me so paranoid that I would begin to hide the drugs and paraphernalia. This went on until the high began to come down. Then I would do it all over again. Sometimes I would get so high I thought I was going to die from a heart attack or indigestion caused by too much gas being trapped in me. Eventually, I got tired of tripping out, so I refused to do cocaine if I didn't have a bag of heroin or some liquor to calm me down.

After Robert found out I had the baby, he came back to New Jersey to see me. I wanted to be with Robert without having to take care of two kids, so I took my son over to my aunt's house so she could keep him for me. She never told me no. She would watch him because she had been crazy about my son ever since I had him. My aunt and my cousin would watch my son for weeks at a time, and they never said a word.

Robert stayed the night with my daughter and me in my hotel room. On this particular night my daughter woke up at 3:00 am in the morning and she wouldn't go back to sleep. She kept crying and crying. I fed her, burped her, and made sure she wasn't wet and she still wouldn't stop crying. Robert kept saying I had spoiled her. It was in the middle of the night and I was very tired. I had been getting up every three hours since I came home from the hospital so I got mad and gave her to her father harshly, rolled over and went to sleep. When I woke up the next morning, my daughter had fallen asleep in her father's arms. This surprised me because Robert had no patience with children. He always refused to watch babies ever since I had known him. He always felt it was a women's job to take care of the children, especially a female child. When I had my daughter, Robert was proud because here he was fifty-six years old with a baby. It made him feel like he still had it going on, and he did!

Robert stayed with me for a couple of days until it was time for him to go back to North Carolina. He gave me money for my daughter and then he left. I couldn't wait until he left because, as soon as he did, the first thing I did was get high. I took my daughter to my twin sister's house, like I always did, so she could watch her. I promised her I would come right back to get my kids, but I never would. Besides, I needed time to recuperate before going back to get them, which usually took two to three days.

Distance Not a Problem

After living in the hotel for several months, my caseworker found another place for me to live. I moved into a house for single mothers with children. I could only live there for a year while I waited for my Section 8 housing voucher to be issued (a Section 8 voucher is given to low-income families to help pay a portion of their rent). Only three families could live in this house located in Bound Brook, NJ. It was a three-story house with three bedrooms on the third floor and a bathroom that we had to share. On the second floor, there was a living room, a dining room, and the kitchen. In the kitchen, we each had an assigned cabinet space and an assigned space in the refrigerator to store our food. The washing machine and dryer were in the basement that we also had to share. The house was very nice.

We had to be in the house at a certain time, and the only time we could stay out all night was on the weekends. Our company couldn't spend the night, and there was an adult at the house to watch us during the daytime. She would leave at about six o'clock in the evening. When she left for the night, we would let our company spend the night, and we never told on each other, so the person in charge of the house never found out. Besides having to keep our rooms clean, we each had our assigned chores every week. The person over us would conduct a daily inspection of our rooms and our assigned chores. Each of us had to open a bank account and put a certain amount of money in the bank each month. This money would be used as a down payment for the security deposit on an apartment. No drugs or alcohol were allowed in the house or in our systems. This rule didn't stop us from drinking in the house after the people left for the day and on the weekend, and I didn't stop using drugs either. I hid my drug use from my roommates; since they weren't street-smart, they couldn't catch me. They were seventeen and eighteen years old, and I was twenty-eight years old.

I would get my welfare check on the first of the month. In the beginning, I put the percentage of money in the bank that was required of me, but as my drug addiction got worse, I would take the money out of the bank little by little until all of it was gone. When the person assigned to us asked where the money was, I told them that my twin sister stole my bankbook and took all of my money out of the bank. I told her I didn't want to prosecute because she was my twin sister, and I didn't want her to get in any trouble. They didn't pursue the matter. They just told me I needed to put the money back in the bank to have for when it was time for me to move.

After living there for a while, I began dating a Caucasian man named Rick. I met him through a bouncer who worked at the bar I went to from time to time. He had a job, so he supported our drug habit. He would come to Bound Brook, pick me up, take me to find a babysitter, and then we would go to his room to get high. I would have sex with him so he would think I really cared about him, but the truth is that having sex with him was disgusting to me, and I did it to get what I wanted from him. Sometimes I would make excuses so I didn't have to have sex with him. Every payday, he would pay his rent, then spend the rest of his money on drugs. After his money was gone, we would wait in his room until someone came who wanted to use his room to get high. They would give him some of their drugs to get high in his room, and he would give me some. After a while, he became stingy, so I had to find my own drugs by prostituting myself.

I began prostituting myself to the man from whom he rented a room. Then I would go back into his room to get high. He didn't care whom I slept with because all he wanted to do was get high too. Eventually, I drifted apart, and he began to see another girl. I didn't care because he would still get me high sometimes.

I began stealing from my roommates. My roommate's boyfriend left money stashed under her mattress. When they left to go out, I arrived home. I was the only person there, so I broke into her room with a knife and took half of the money, then called a cab and went to my Caucasian friend's house to get high. She didn't know who had taken the money because I wasn't there when she left, and I wasn't there when she came home. When I arrived home and she mentioned the money to me, I acted surprised, and I acted as if I were trying to help figure out who had taken the money. She couldn't say anything to the people managing the house because the money was drug money, and her boyfriend had no business there, anyway.

Another time, I stole my other roommate's food stamps. I lay on my bed and pretended I was asleep as I waited for her to take a shower. As soon as she went into the bathroom, I shut the door, eased off my bed, tiptoed into her room, and quickly took the food stamps out of her purse. Then I hurried back into my room, eased back onto my bed, and pretended I was asleep. When she realized her food stamps were gone, I acted like I didn't know what she was talking about, assured her that I didn't take them, and accused our other roommate of taking them. She acted like she believed me. Then we began talking about our roommate behind her back. I waited until later that night, put my children to bed, and asked the same girl from whom I had taken the food stamps if she could keep an eye on my children until I came back. I went to the phone booth, called my Caucasian friend, and asked him if he could come take me to sell the food stamps so we could get some drugs. After he picked me up we took my children to my twin sister's house, and then we took off to get high. I stayed gone for several days.

I remember one particular day when I wanted to get high really badly, but I didn't have any money. I put my children to bed, then left home, walking toward New Brunswick. Bound Brook, NJ, was about twenty-five minutes' driving distance from New Brunswick. It would have taken me half the night to get to New Brunswick on foot, so I decided to go to a phone booth and call the cops to get a ride. I told them I was stranded because the guy I was with put me out of his car because I didn't want to have sex with him. When the police officer took the police report, he asked me what the guy looked like and what type of car he was driving. I gave the officer a phony description of a person and a description of a phony car. The cop asked me where I lived, and I told him I lived on Townsend St. in New Brunswick (that's where my Caucasian friend lived). He then told me to get into the car, and he would take me home. When I got into the police car the officer radioed to the dispatcher and told him he was leaving his jurisdiction to take me home. He took me right to the spot where I wanted to go.

My drug habit continued to get worse. I began stealing things from the house where I lived. Agencies would donate items to the program I was in to help people who were in need. The person who was in charge of the house where I lived stored the things in the attic before I moved in. The entrance to the attic was in my bedroom. I would let down the ladder and climb up into the attic, take items I knew would sell, then go sell them and buy some cocaine. I did that until all the good stuff was gone. No one ever found out because they never checked up in the attic while I lived there.

When my year was up to live in the house, I had to move out. My Section Eight voucher hadn't been issued yet, nor had I saved any money for an apartment, so I had to ask my aunt if I could come to live with her. She said yes and let me stay in one of her bedrooms for a small fee. I let my son go stay with one of my other aunts and her daughter because the room this aunt rented to me was too small. I didn't have the patience to deal with two children at the time. My aunt and my cousin were crazy about my son so they didn't mind.

I appreciated my aunt for letting me stay with her, but the house was always dirty because she didn't take the time to teach her children how to clean. I had to clean the bathroom and kitchen every time I wanted to use them. As soon as I cleaned them, her children would go right behind me and dirty them up again. My aunt's kids were so lazy and nasty that she would give me "drugs" to clean the house for her. I promised the Lord that if He let my Section 8 voucher come through, I would never live with anyone else because I was tired of living in filth. I stayed with my aunt until my Section 8 voucher was approved. I was so happy because now I could get my own apartment and keep it clean.

I only had two months to find an apartment before my Section Eight voucher would expire. I looked and looked, and time was running out. The only thing I could find was a two-bedroom attic apartment in New Brunswick. The Board of Social Services gave me a month and a half's security for the apartment and a voucher to buy furniture. The attic apartment was cold in the winter and very hot in the summer, but I dealt with it because, at least, it was mine.

While I was living there I met a guy who was an alcoholic. When he came to my house he would be so drunk that he would pass out. After he would pass out I would go through his pants pockets, take his money then leave him and my daughter in the house asleep while I went to get my drugs.

At first, I hid my drug use from him, but eventually, I couldn't hide it anymore, so I ended up telling him about it. He didn't like drugs, but he would give me money anyway to buy them; however, sometimes he would get mad and tell me he wasn't going to give me any money. Of course, I wasn't trying to hear that, so I would keep asking him for the money until he gave it to me. Sometimes, we would end up having a heated argument, and he would leave.

Some days, I would take my kids to my twin sister's house if I wanted to get high, but most of the time, I stayed home and got high after they went to sleep. I didn't like getting high while they were awake because the least little noise would get on my nerves.

Again, I couldn't understand back then why I smoked crack because every time I smoked it, I would hear noises and become paranoid. It made me think someone was watching me when there wasn't. I would turn off the lights, turn down the music, and get really quiet as if I were trying to hide from someone or something. After my high would come down, I would look on the floor for pieces of cocaine that I thought I had dropped when I hadn't. I would even accuse the person who gave me the cocaine of stealing from me. I began snorting heroin before I would smoke crack because the cocaine would make me so paranoid that I had to have something to calm me down. I would continue getting high until I couldn't find any more ways to get high, or I would just pass out.

Lord, You Are the Only One Who Can Help Me!

I couldn't take the heat in the attic apartment during the summer, so I decided to move. I found an apartment on Baldwin Street in New Brunswick. This was the worst move I could make in my life because drug addicts and drug dealers hung out on every corner, and there were bars on every corner, too.

My drug addiction progressed even more, and I began using drugs every day. I started letting people who didn't have anywhere to get high come into my house and do their drugs, but they had to share with me. They liked coming to my house because I didn't allow more than three to four people in at a time. If I allowed more than four people in my house at a time, I would get paranoid, and I would ask them to leave.

My children started school; my son was in kindergarten, and my daughter went to daycare, so I would try to get as high as I could while they weren't there. I would snort some heroin to come down before I had to go pick them up.

I always kept my children well-dressed and their hair well-groomed so people in the area wouldn't think my drug habit was as bad as it was. What I also tried to hide from them was that I would abuse my son. After I got high off cocaine, I would always think my son was doing something he had no business doing, so I would punch, bite, or slap him. I began treating him really badly. After I came down off my high, I would feel really bad for what I did to him, so I would go into his bedroom and tell him I was sorry, but I would always tell him he shouldn't have done what he did. My son had a really hard time growing up. I always treated my daughter better than him. Until this day, I don't know why I mistreated my son because he was a good child, and he never really gave me any trouble. He was always very sad.

My mother realized I was abusing him, so she called the Division of Youth and Family Services on me. When they came to my house, I told them I did abuse him; I got his coat and told them I thought it would be best if they took him until I got myself together. They checked my son for physical marks of abuse on his body; they didn't find any, and then they checked the refrigerator and cabinets to see if there was food. I had plenty of food, so they decided not to take him. I was very disappointed because I was tired of abusing my son and I felt he would have been better off somewhere else.

I was tired of using drugs, so I signed myself into the hospital to detoxify. I stayed there for one week, then the hospital released me and let me go home. After I came home, my boyfriend felt it was safe enough for him to come and live with me because he thought I was through using drugs. I stayed clean for a couple of days, and then I was right back to using drugs again. I had tried so many times to quit using drugs only to fail, so I started believing this was the way God created me to be. I began telling people that I was the best drug addict. I remember someone telling me that the best drug addicts were "six feet under."

I had to hide my drug use from my boyfriend because he began trying to watch every move I made. The girl who lived upstairs from me sold drugs, so I didn't have to leave the house to get high. As soon as my boyfriend would leave the house, I would go right up the back stairs and get my drugs. I would sneak a hit, then go back to cleaning or something, as if I were doing nothing. My boyfriend would try to double back to the house and catch me, but he never could. After a while, I got tired of deceiving him, so I told him that I had started getting high again. He didn't like it, but what could he do? Again, he tried not to give me money for drugs, but I always talked him into it anyway.

One day, I wanted to get high really badly, so I begged him to give me money for drugs. At first, he said no, and then he said that he would give me the money to buy some cocaine, but he warned that the minute I started tripping out, he was going to slap the taste out of my mouth. After getting the drugs from the girl who lived upstairs from me, I took my first hit and began looking in the garbage for pieces of cocaine that I thought I had dropped in there. Of course, I didn't drop any pieces of rock cocaine in the garbage, so my boyfriend got up from the table and slapped me so hard that my cheek burned for about five minutes. I got mad and hit him back, so we began to fight. He was getting the best of me, so I ran around the house so he couldn't get me. I then ran out of the front door and came back into the house through the back door. I opened the kitchen cabinet, took out a bottle of bleach real fast, and poured some into a small cup. When he came in the back door after me, I told him that if he came any closer, I was going to throw the bleach in his eyes. He didn't believe me, so he proceeded to come toward me. I threw the bleach right in his eyes and ran back outside through the front door as he tried to follow me. I then ran back into the house through the back door again. By this time, he was outside, so I locked both doors so he couldn't get back into the house. He proceeded to knock on the door, but I wouldn't let him in because I was scared. I thought he was going to kill me for throwing bleach in his eyes. A few moments went by, then he left. About a half hour later, he returned with his friend. His friend knocked and knocked on the door for me to let them in, but I refused. Finally, he told me Lee couldn't see out of his eyes and that he needed to go to the hospital. I felt sorry for him, so I opened the door and let them in. When I opened the door, my boyfriend had his hands over his eyes because he really couldn't see. My boyfriend's friend stayed at the house to watch my children, who were asleep in their room while I walked my boyfriend to the hospital.

The doctor asked what happened, and I told him. They washed his eyes out and then gave him some eye solution to take home so he could continue to wash his eyes out continuously for three days. During those three days, I had to wait on him for his every need. After three days, his eyesight began to come back. He and I joked about what had happened after his eyesight returned, but deep down inside, I knew he would never forget what I had done to him. After that, he and I began to fight all the time, so I told him he had to leave my home. He said he would come back to get his things, but I was so mad that I threw all of his things outside on the curb. After a while, I tried to get him to move his things back into my apartment, but he wouldn't. He would only spend the night. He said, "A woman only has one chance to throw my belongings out. I will never live with her again."

After a while, he and I began to drift apart, and he started seeing another woman, but he still came to see me, and we would even have sex from time to time. I liked when he came over, especially when he was drunk because I could go through his pockets and take his money after he passed out. I began to use heroin more often. I had to have a bag of heroin to begin my day. Sometimes when he came to see me, he didn't have any money, so I would beg him to go and do an odd job or something so he could buy me a bag of heroin. After he bought me the bag of heroin, I would try to find a way to get some crack cocaine. I did this every day, all day. Some days I would be so tired from getting high for two days at a time that I would sleep until my body was rested; then I would begin the same routine again.

On the first of the month, when I received my welfare check, I would take my rent money and half of my food stamps and give them to a friend of mine to hold, so I wouldn't spend them all on drugs. I always kept my rent paid, and most of the time, I kept food in the house for my kids.

One month, I spent all of my food stamps and the money I had left, after I paid my rent, on drugs. As a result, my kids didn't have any food. The next day, my kids came to me to tell me they were hungry. I told them to leave me alone, even as I lay on the couch in the dark, depressed and worried about how I was going to feed them. It bothered me to see my children hungry and not be able to feed them.

As I lay on the couch, I asked God what I was going to do and if He could please help me. About an hour later, I heard a knock at the door. When I answered the door, it was my landlord. He had a crate of food in his hand. He told me he was giving out food at church and that the Lord had laid it on his heart to bring me some food. I was so happy! I took the food and thanked him. I knew God was looking out for my children and me. When I closed the door, I said, "Thank you, Jesus!" for providing food for me and my children. It was enough food to last until I received more food stamps on the first of the month.

On the first of the month, when I got my welfare check, I

began playing the pick-it. One day, I played the pick four straight and box, and I hit. It paid three thousand seven hundred dollars. Boy, was I happy! I went to the store to cash the ticket in, but no store in my area had enough money to cash it, so I paid a guy to take me to the liquor store in Somerset to cash the ticket in. After I got the money, I went to the store and bought a VCR and a stereo. I took a couple of hundred out to buy me some drugs, then I gave the rest of my money to a trust worthy friend to hold it for me so I wouldn't spend it up all on drugs.

I paid for a babysitter, bought my heroin, then I went and got my best friend, and we locked ourselves in my apartment and started getting high. If someone knocked on the door, we didn't answer it because now we didn't need anyone to get us high; we had enough drugs to last us a couple of days. After the drugs were all gone, I called the person I let hold my money so he could bring me some more money to buy more drugs. I gave my sister more money so she could watch my children longer for me and I began getting high again.

I began doing two bags of heroin and smoking as much cocaine as I wanted. I continued to do this until all my money was gone. By the time all my money was gone, I was doing three bags of heroin and smoking even more cocaine a day. I was so strung out on heroin that I couldn't get out of bed unless I had a bag. I would be so sick that I would vomit, and my bones would ache. I needed a bag of heroin to be able to get out of bed, another one so I wouldn't feel sick, and the third one so I could get high.

One day, this guy came to my house to get high. Because I was so sick from not having heroin, he felt sorry for me. He threw a bag of heroin on my bed and told me to get up then went into the kitchen to get high off of crack cocaine alone. I was so sick I couldn't even get up to snort the bag of heroin he gave me. I just slid it under my pillow and went back to sleep. When I woke up the next day, I snorted the heroin, then dressed my kids for school. If I woke up sick and didn't have a bag of heroin, I wouldn't send my kids to school. I would make them stay home, especially if I didn't have clean clothes for them to wear.

After I spent all my money, I sold my VCR and stereo so I could buy some drugs. I sold each item for much less than what I had paid for them. I didn't care because all I wanted to do was get high.

After I sold everything in my apartment that was worth selling, I began prostituting my body for money. I would walk up and down Commercial Avenue until whoever wanted to buy sex stopped to pick me up. We would ride around for a few minutes while we negotiated a price, then we would park the car somewhere in a secluded area while we had intercourse or while I performed oral sex on him, whichever he preferred. I hated prostituting, but that was the only way I knew of at the time I could get money to buy some drugs.

Some of the men who picked me up didn't like using condoms. When I asked them if they wanted to use a condom, they would say no. I would be sarcastic with them by saying, "Oh, you're so sure I'm clean and healthy, huh?" They would say I didn't look like I had anything wrong with me and that I looked like a clean person. I would remind them that a person can't tell if something is wrong with someone or not just by looking at them; then I would make them go somewhere to buy a condom. Not only did I want them to wear a condom because I knew I was HIV positive; I didn't know if they had a disease, and using a condom made it somewhat easier for me to have sex with a man I didn't love. I didn't have to come in contact with his bodily fluids. If I didn't love a man, when he ejaculated his sperm, it was disgusting to me.

I started getting scared to walk the streets alone at night, trying to pick up men for money because prostitutes were being murdered, so I began stealing from stores to support my drug habit. A guy would drive me and another lady to a store to steal baby Pampers and Enfamil. I would take my daughter to the store with me so I wouldn't look suspicious. As I pushed my daughter in the carriage, I would fill the carriage with lots of milk and Pampers; then I would push her out of the store without paying for the items. We would take the milk and Pampers to a store owned by Puerto Ricans and sell them at a cheaper price than they would have to pay a vendor.

I thought about the consequences I would have to face if I got caught stealing. Not only would I have gone to jail, but my kids would be in the custody of the Division of Youth and Family Services and placed in a foster home. At the time, I didn't care because I was sick, and all I wanted to do was get high so I could feel better.

I couldn't continue taking that risk, so I started calling drug dealers up and inviting them to my house so I could perform sexual acts with them for drugs. Sometimes I would have sex with two men, one right after the other, just for a couple of bags of cocaine that only lasted maybe three to four hours if I smoked them alone. After I came down from my high, I thought about the embarrassing things I did to get high and the things I did while I was high. I felt so embarrassed about what I had done that I would go into a state of depression, but as soon as I needed to get high again, I would do the same thing. I was tired of living the way I was, but I didn't know what to do or whom to turn to for help. I had tried rehab, and it didn't help me. People would say, "If you really wanted to quit, you could," but that wasn't true. I wanted to stop so badly, but I just couldn't.

There were days when my children had to miss school

because I would oversleep, or I would be too sick to get up and dress them. Sometimes they didn't have clean clothes to put on because I spent all the laundry money on drugs, and I wouldn't take the time to wash their clothes by hand.

If the lady upstairs didn't have any drugs, I would either ask her to listen out for my children, or I would just leave them in the house by themselves while I went to buy my drugs. Even though I was on drugs really badly, I loved my children, and I was determined not to give up trying to take care of them. I was tired of abusing my children. I was tired of being sick from not having drugs and of trying to find money to support my drug habit, so I signed myself into another detox hospital. I stayed in the hospital for seven days, when I came home I put signs on my door saying, "Please do not bring drugs to my home."

My boyfriend and I began to see each other again; he was glad I was not using drugs, so we got along well. He tried to keep me happy by having cookouts while we listened to oldies music at my house. He made sure he had beer and liquor because he was an alcoholic, but he didn't think his problem was worse than mine.

Drinking didn't satisfy me; it only made me want to get high off of cocaine and heroin. After about two weeks, I started using drugs behind my boyfriend's back. When my boyfriend would leave the house, he would try to sneak back to see if he could catch me, but he couldn't catch me because I would watch out for him through the windows and hide the drugs and pipe when I saw him coming. I would always outsmart him, and I hid my drug use from him for as long as I could.

One day, my boyfriend, his friends, and I were at my boyfriend's rented room. We were drinking, and I wanted some cocaine, so I asked my boyfriend if he could buy me some. He said, "No," so I left to find some money to buy some or someone to get me high. After I got high, I wanted some more, so I went back to my boyfriend's room to ask him to buy me some. When I asked him, he got mad, and we ended up getting into a fight. He started hitting me, so I ran out of the house. He ran after me and caught me in an alleyway. He beat me so badly I thought my ribs were cracked, and he also gave me a black eye. He made me go back into the house. When I got in the house, I ran into his room and locked the door so he couldn't hit me anymore. My boyfriend put his landlord's pit bull outside the room so I wouldn't come out. I was so mad that I took my boyfriend's drill that he had in his closet and drilled holes in all of his walls, and I threw his television out the window. My boyfriend got mad and called the cops. He waited until he thought the cops arrived at the house, then he put the pit bull back in his roommate's room. Before the cops came into the house, I ran out of the room, ran into the kitchen, got a knife, and stuck it straight through my boyfriend's leg before pulling it out. When the cops came into the house, my boyfriend told them I stabbed him with a knife, drilled holes in his walls, and threw his T.V. out of the window. The cops asked me if I had stabbed my boyfriend, and I told them yes and the reason why. The cops told me I was under arrest for assault. They put handcuffs on me and placed me in the back seat of the patrol car. I was upset because they weren't going to lock my boyfriend up for beating me, so I told the cops my boyfriend had a warrant out for his arrest for unpaid child support. The police did a background check on him and found what I said to be true, so they arrested my boyfriend and then put him in the back seat of the other patrol car. I stayed in jail one night and was let out the next day without paying bail. My boyfriend stayed in jail for a month. When I got my welfare check, his friend and I bailed him out.

One night, I decided to give my five-year-old daughter a bath. While my daughter's bathwater was running, I put her in the tub. I put in just enough water to cover her bottom. I turned the water off to go into the kitchen to get something from the refrigerator. As I was standing at the door of the refrigerator, I passed out. I didn't wake up until my daughter got out of the tub and came to wake me up. She said, "Mommy, I was in the tub a long time." I don't know how long I was out, but when I realized what had happened, I went to check the bathwater. It was cold, so I must have been out a good while. I was so glad I had only put a little water in the bathtub because my daughter could have drowned.

The police had been watching the lady upstairs because she was a drug dealer. The day the police raided her house, they found lots of cocaine and heroin. They took her to jail, and because she had a lot of drugs, her bail was pretty high. She couldn't make bail, so she had to sit in jail until someone came up with enough money to bail her out. While she was locked up all of my ways and schemes for getting drugs began to run out, so I became desperate. I decided to break into her apartment and steal some of her belongings that would sell so that I could buy some drugs.

To get to her door upstairs, I had to go out of my inside back door, then walk up her back stairs from inside the house so no one could see me when I went up to her apartment.

The first time I broke into her apartment, I used a butter knife. I went through her things and took stuff that was small enough to carry so no one would notice her things were missing. I had to be careful because the people who lived across the street from us were keeping an eye on the lady's apartment. They knew a lot of drug users came to the house, and they didn't want anyone to break in and steal her things. They had no idea I was the one they had to watch out for.

When the lady upstairs came home from jail and found her things missing, she asked me if I had seen anyone go into her apartment. I told her that I had heard lots of people going upstairs, knocking on the door to buy drugs, but I didn't open the door to see who they were. I think she had an idea I broke into her apartment, but she couldn't prove it. She called the cops and reported that her apartment had been broken into, but the police didn't care because she was a drug dealer with a record. She changed her old locks and replaced them with a pad lock thinking it would be better.

Going to jail didn't stop her from selling drugs. As a matter of fact, she continued to sell drugs, and she ended up getting raided again and going back to jail. This time, she stayed locked up for a long time because her bail was too high for anyone she knew to get her out.

I needed some drugs really badly, and I didn't have any money, nor would anyone give me any, so I decided to break into the lady's upstairs apartment again. This time, I couldn't use a butter knife to get into her apartment because of the padlock on her door. The only other way I could get in was to kick her door in, so that's what I did. I kicked her door in and took what I wanted.

I told a guy friend of mine what I had done. I also told him what the lady had left in her apartment because I wanted him to help me lift the heavy stuff out of her apartment. We waited until it was very late and dark outside; then we went back into her apartment, took her stereo, washing machine, jewelry, and all of her babies' clothes. Some still had tags on them. She bought most of her belonging from drug addicts who had stolen them from the store and exchanged the items for drugs, so we felt it served her right to steal it back from her.

After I smoked crack I always became very paranoid and nervous especially since the cops had busted the lady upstairs for selling drugs. Perhaps the fact that I had broke into her apartment and stole most of her things made me that way. I would bug out so bad that I would turn off all the lights in the house, peek through the windows trying to see if there were police or unmarked cars around the house. I would even lay flat on the floor, on my belly and look underneath the door to see if anyone was standing on the other side of the door waiting to burst it open. Sometimes I would even take all the drugs and paraphernalia off the table and hide it believing I heard someone coming. People started thinking I was going crazy and they didn't feel comfortable getting high with me any more so most of them stopped coming to my apartment to get high.

I was tired of being sick and looking for ways to get high, so I decided that I needed a change. I felt that if I moved out of the drug area, I would stop using drugs, so I told my landlord I would be moving out of the apartment in two months, even though I hadn't found an apartment yet. In the meantime, I hadn't stopped getting high, so I was never in any shape to look for an apartment. A month went by, and I still hadn't found another apartment to live in.

One night, I was home alone, sitting at my kitchen table getting high, and I started thinking about how many times I had tried to stop using drugs and how many times I had been to rehab. I knew going back to rehab wasn't going to help me. I started thinking about the things my grandmother taught me about the Lord. My grandmother trusted in God, and she instilled her beliefs in me. I had a crack pipe, cooked crack, cigarettes, and matches sitting on my table when I hung my head down and said, "Lord, I've tried everything I know of that I thought could help me to stop using drugs, and nothing has worked." I said, "Lord, You are going to have to take this addiction away from me." The Lord told me to get my Bible and start reading in the book of Revelation. I turned to Revelation chapters 19-20 and started reading about the "bottomless pit and the lake of fire and how Satan and all those who didn't want to live right would burn forever and ever." I began to cry as I told the Lord that I didn't want to die and go to hell. I left everything on my kitchen table and went into my bedroom and cried until I fell asleep. That night, God dealt with me mightily.

The next morning, when the Lord woke me up, He told me to go get a newspaper and look for an apartment, so I did. There was an ad in the newspaper for an available two-bedroom apartment, and the landlord accepted tenants who were on the Section Eight housing program. I called the landlord and told him about my drug use and that I wanted to move from the area I was living in because it was a drug area, and I wanted to change my life. The landlord said he would talk to his wife, give me a call back, or I could call him back the next day. I said, "Okay, thank you," then I hung up the phone. The next day, I called the landlord's house, and his wife answered the phone. I talked to her for about an hour, telling her about myself, my drug use, and how I wanted to stop using drugs and move out of the drug area where I lived. I also told her how I felt and my future plans. She said she would talk to her husband and get back to me. They did get back to me and they decided to take a chance on me and let me rent the apartment.

All transactions that involved paperwork were done through the mail. I took the papers that I needed the landlord to fill out over to the house he was going to rent to me and put them in the mailbox. He filled them out, signed them, and put them back in the mailbox; then I would pick them up. I didn't lay eyes on my landlord until one year after moving into the apartment. I know it was God who gave me favor and who was turning my life around because of the way everything was happening.

My mother came to my house one Friday while I was still living on Baldwin St. in New Brunswick to tell me that Pastor

Elois Bellamy, the pastor of Deliverance Prayer Revival Tabernacle, was having church service under the tent at the park across the street from the house where I lived. She asked my girlfriend and me if we wanted to go. We said yes, so she waited until we got dressed, and then we went across the street to the church. My mother didn't know my girlfriend and I were high on heroin, and not only that, I had the rest of it in my pocket and was on my way to church with it. Even though I was high, I knew I needed help and that God was the only one who could deliver me from my drug addiction.

I was tired of the life I was living; I was tired of depending on heroin to help me to be able function from day to day and from being sick when I couldn't get the drug. I was tired of abusing and neglecting my children. I was tired of people seeing me look bad and tired of people putting me down by calling me a drug addict and not trusting me. I was tired of selling my body to get drugs and I was tired of people using me for sex then brushing me off like I was nothing. I was miserable and slowly dying and I wanted all this to stop.

As I was sitting in the front row of the church, I noticed a guy in a wheelchair, who had both of his legs amputated, being pushed to the front of the church, close to the altar. To my surprise, it was a gentleman I dated for a short time when I lived on Baldwin St. When I saw him, I was shocked and became deeply troubled as tears filled my eyes, and I began to feel sorry for him. Seeing him in that condition made me think about life and how short it is. I began to think about my own life and the way I was living. Reality began to set in, and I realized that anything could happen to me while living the way I was.

As Pastor Bellamy brought forth the Word of God, the spirit of God began to convict me, and I started crying out to God. I took the heroin out of my pocket, threw it on the ground, and smashed it. During the altar call, I went up for prayer, and Pastor Bellamy had me say the "sinner's prayer," then she prayed the prayer of faith over me. My mother began to give God praise because I had given my life to the Lord.

After church, my uncle, who also attended the service, came up to me and said, "You know that wasn't heroin you smashed on the ground; you know it was only baby powder." He said it to be funny, but I told him no, it wasn't; it was the real thing. When her high went down, my girlfriend got mad at me for smashing the heroin on the ground. After church, she left me to go back under the tent to see if she could find the drugs. Later that night, my high wore off too, and I started to feel bad for smashing the heroin on the ground. I thought about going out to find money or drugs so I could get high again, but because it was late, I just went to bed.

The next night, there was another church service being held under the tent, and even though my old way of thinking continued to torment me, it didn't stop me from attending the church service because I desperately wanted to be delivered from drugs. As I sat in my seat, all I could think about was the altar call because I was going right back up for prayer, knowing I wasn't delivered yet. Since I had gone to the altar the night before to repent of my sins and to accept Jesus Christ as my personal Savior, Pastor Bellamy said, "If you came to the altar last night, you don't need to come again because you are already saved through faith." She also said God heard us and had forgiven us. I knew she was talking to me, but that didn't stop me from going back up for prayer because I wanted God to deliver me from drugs. God touched me that night, and I danced all around the tent. When I left church that night I didn't feel the same because God was delivering me.

As days went by, I tried my hardest not to get high, but

people would come by my apartment to ask me to get high, and eventually, I did because I wasn't strong enough to resist.

The kids and I were very excited about moving to Somerset. I told the kids about the positive things we could do and gain from our move. I explained to them that there were several parks we could go to, and one of them had a swimming pool. I also promised them I would take them to one of the parks as soon as we had settled in.

Two months prior, I had given a friend of mine permission to live with me, so she was moving to Somerset with us as well. My girlfriend was a heavy drinker, and she also smoked crack cocaine. She would hang out with other alcoholics for two to three days at a time, and when she got tired, she would come and rest for two or three days. When she was at the house, she made sure the house was clean. She would cook and even spend time with the kids, taking them outside for walks to the park. Then she would go on another drinking binge that lasted for three to four days. I didn't like people staying with me because I was scared my Section 8 worker would find out and kick me off the program. Because she helped keep the house clean and was hardly ever there, I took a chance and let her stay with me.

Time was drawing nigh for me to move from Baldwin Street to Hamilton St. in Somerset, NJ. The only time I could pack was when I was high on heroin and cocaine. I would stay up all night packing and getting high until my body couldn't take any more abuse from the lack of sleep. I would pass out for a night and a day, then I was right back to getting high and packing.

As I began to put my belongings on the back of the truck, I realized I had a problem. The people across the street were keeping an eye on the lady's apartment upstairs because the lady was still locked up. My neighbors were sitting on their front porch, watching me move. I didn't want them to see the washing machine that I had stolen from the lady upstairs because I was afraid they would recognize it wasn't mine and call the police. So I covered the washing machine with a sheet and put it in the back of the truck. Then I hurried up and piled other things on top of it. They didn't notice, so I got away with stealing the washing machine.

I liked the apartment in Somerset because it was in a better neighborhood, newly painted, and the carpet was new. The outside of the house needed a lot of work done on it, but that didn't matter to me. All that mattered was that the kids and I were going to be living in a drug-free environment.

After I moved all my belongings into my new apartment, I knew I needed to at least get the bed up so the kids and I would have something to sleep on. I didn't want the children to be in the way, so I gave my girlfriend, whom I let live with me, two dollars in food stamps, and I gave each of my children a dollar for ice cream. I figured since my girlfriend had just come off a drinking binge a day ago, she wouldn't be drinking for a couple of days. I still reminded her not to drink while she had my children, but she didn't do what I asked her. She took my children to the park, then she left the park and went to her sister's house, which didn't live far from the park. Her sister was an alcoholic, too. When my friend got to her sister's house, she and her friends were drinking alcohol. My friend joined in and got really drunk. It started raining when my children and she began walking home. My children got soaking wet, and on top of that, my friend was mean to them. She was pulling and hitting them because they couldn't walk as fast as she wanted them to. Policemen were driving by and happened to see her abusing my children, so they pulled over to check on them. They realized my friend was very intoxicated, so they arrested her for endangering a minor. After finding out my children were not hers, the policemen asked her where they lived so they could bring them to me. She showed them where I lived and they brought my children to the house.

I had been up all night getting high and packing prior to my move to our new apartment. After putting up the kids' bunk bed and my full-size bed, I took a shower, then I lay across my bed to rest. I was so tired that I fell into a deep sleep. When the police came to the house to bring the children, I didn't hear them knocking on the door, so they took my kids to the police station to get information from them about the next of kin. My kids were too young, so they couldn't provide any information about my family members. The policemen had to take them to the Division of Family Services office in Edison, NJ. Later that evening, my caseworker from Family Services brought the kids back to see if I was there. I was still sound asleep, so I didn't hear her knocking on the door either; she left a note telling me the Division of Youth and Family Services had custody of my children. Because it was getting late in the evening and I hadn't called the Youth and Family Service, she placed my children in a temporary foster home. After I woke up I found the note that was left telling me where my children were, but by the time I woke up the office was closed, so I had to wait until the next morning to try to find out information about my children. The next morning, I went to a phone booth and called the Youth and Family Service office. I asked them if they had my children. They said yes, but they couldn't tell me where they were until they investigated my drug use and living arrangements. Even though I had just moved into a new apartment and my living arrangements were fine, I knew I had a problem with drugs and that it was going to keep me from getting my children back. I became very worried and depressed.

Deep down inside, I loved my children, and I didn't want anyone to raise them but me. I always felt no one could love or take care of them better than I could. Having my children kept me from being able to run the streets. When I think about it, my children were a blessing to me. Because of my drug addiction, I was unable to keep a job, but because I had children, I was able to get public assistance to support us.

As I was sitting in my house thinking about my children and the possibility of me never being able to see them again, I got depressed. The devil told me to close all the blinds, turn off all the lights, get in the bed, don't open the door for anyone and that's what I did.

As I was lying in my bed with the covers over my head, the Lord spoke to me and told me to get up and go tell my mother what happened to my children so she could try to help me get them back. When God spoke to me, it was as if a light went on inside me. I jumped up, walked about seven blocks to where my mother was, and explained to her what happened. My mother called my caseworker at the Youth and Family Service office and spoke with her. My caseworker gave my mother and me an appointment to come see her.

The following week, we took a train to Edison, NJ, to speak with my caseworker. My mother didn't like the fact that I was on drugs, so she told my caseworker about my drug addiction to try to get me the help I needed. My mother told my caseworker she was willing to take custody of my children until I got the help I needed, but she needed somewhere for us to live because the lady my mother lived with had several kids of her own and her apartment was too small and already over crowded for all of us to live there long term.

My family service worker made arrangements with my Section Eight housing case worker for my mother to live in my apartment with my children until I came home from rehab and regained custody of my children. My mother explained to me that the only way she would watch my children was if I agreed to go to an in-patient rehabilitation facility for six months. Since I had already been to several thirty-day in-patient programs, she felt staying in an in-patient program longer was the only way I would get the help I needed. When I heard this, I became very upset because I didn't want to go to any more in-patient programs, and I definitely didn't want to stay in one longer than thirty days, so I said I wasn't going to go. After my caseworker checked my mother's living arrangements and they checked out okay, my children were released to my mother's care.

My caseworker told my mother that my children were not to go anywhere with me alone and that I could only visit my children while we were in her company. When I got high, part of me was glad my mother had custody of my children because now I had nothing holding me back from getting high. I could go and come as I pleased. I didn't have to worry about taking my children with me to buy my drugs or who was going to watch them. Each time I finished getting high, reality would set in, and then I would begin to miss my children. I didn't like the fact that I wasn't there to raise my children myself, so I decided to take my mother's offer and go to rehab for six months.

When I left for rehab, my mother moved into my apartment with my children. I told my mother when she moved into my apartment to leave my room vacant. I asked her not to bother my things in my room because I wanted it to stay as it was. I also let her know she was more than welcome to take the living room and use it as her bedroom.

I was responsible for finding a rehabilitation facility to go into, but as I called around to each facility, I found out they were all full, and it would be several weeks before I could get into one. So, while I waited, I continued to get high.

One day, I wanted to get high really badly. I didn't have any money, and no one would come to my apartment to get me high, so I decided to try to get some money by prostituting my body.

I never liked prostituting in the daytime because I was scared someone I knew would see me. I would always wait until it was night to go out and solicit my body. I walked from Somerset to New Brunswick to get to Commercial Avenue, where most of the men drove around to pick up women.

Three men in a van who moved to the United States from another country stopped to pick me up because they wanted to buy sex. When the van stopped and I saw there were three men in the van, I was kind of scared to get in, but they convinced me they weren't going to hurt me, so I decided to get in the van and go with them.

One of the men asked me if I knew of anyone else who was willing to go out with him, so we went to a lady's house whom I thought would be willing to date him, but she wasn't home. I decided to go with them to their apartment alone.

All three men wanted sex, so I decided to have sex with all of them; in return, they paid me thirty dollars apiece. Each man had his turn. When one was done, the next man would come into the room and have his turn. The only sensible thing we did right was use a condom. Out of all three, I found one of them to be more caring than the others, so I continued to see him.

He knew I got high, so he would buy drugs for me sometimes, but sometimes he would tell me I didn't need the stuff. When he wouldn't give me money to buy drugs, I would wait until he was asleep, then steal his money and his car keys to go buy some drugs. He got tired of me stealing his money, so he began hiding his wallet in the van before coming into my apartment. When he did this, I would steal his keys to the van, go outside, and try to find his wallet. I could never find his money because he would hide his wallet underneath the van's rear tire somewhere. I found this out because I watched him from my apartment window as he left and I saw him bend down near the rear tire to get his wallet.

Several days went by, and I hadn't seen him. I didn't know what was wrong until one day, one of his friends came to my apartment and told me that he had had a tragic accident. He told me that my friend had gone out to a bar and somehow ended up at someone's house, where he had fallen or had been pushed off of a two-story building. Someone told the police my friend had fallen off the roof of the building, but my friend's friend said that my friend didn't know anyone at the apartment building where he fell. The whole incident was suspicious.

His friend and I went to the hospital to see him, and he was in very bad shape. He came in and out of consciousness. He was bleeding from his ears, and the bones under the bottoms of both his feet were cracked. Seeing my friend lying in the hospital made me realize how much I really cared about him. I cried for him because I hated seeing him in that condition.

Even though I wasn't saved at the time, I knew the only person who could help him was God, so I went to my cousin, Tina, and asked her if she would go to the hospital with me and pray for him. She said she would, so we went to the hospital the same day, and she prayed for him. I knew he was going to be all right after that.

I could only visit him one more time before leaving for rehab. As I held his hand and talked to him, he squeezed my hand. That was his way of letting me know he knew who I was, and I felt much better knowing that.

The police told us that after he got better, he would be deported back to his country because his visa had run out and he was in the United States illegally.

Even though I was scheduled to go to rehab, I continued to get high every day. Again, I needed drugs really badly, and I didn't have any money to buy them. It was time for the kids to go back to school, so I decided to go to this lady's house I used to live next door to on Baldwin Street in New Brunswick. I asked her what kind of clothing she needed for her children who were about to go back to school. She told me she needed some boy's underwear, so I went downtown to a store, stole them for her, and then sold them to her at a cheaper price than what the store would charge. After she brought the underwear I went to the drug dealer and brought a vial of cocaine and a bag of heroin.

I bought the drugs from someone I didn't know, so the heroin was very weak, and the cocaine wasn't very good either. I decided to go back to the person I had bought the drugs from, but he had left to go get high himself after ripping me off. I was so mad, but there was nothing I could do about it, so I decided to go back to the same store to steal some more underwear.

On my way into the store, I noticed my mother going into Burger King across the street. I didn't say anything to her because I didn't want her to see me.

I went into the store, and as I was putting the underwear in the plastic bag, I noticed a lady who worked at the store watching me. I tried to act like I wasn't doing anything. I figured she had caught on to what I was doing, so I headed for the door to leave the store before she could stop me. As I headed for the door, the lady told me to stop, but I wouldn't. I started running, so the lady screamed out, "Catch that girl; she has a bag of underwear!" I ran out of the door with the bag of underwear in my hand. I figured if I ran down by the courthouse, the police wouldn't think to look for me there, so that's what I did. I was one block away from the courthouse when a police car pulled up to the corner where I was standing. The policemen asked me what was in the bag I was holding. I told them I didn't know; some girl asked me to hold the bag for her. They asked me which way the girl went, and as I pointed up the street, they told me to get into the police car so we could go and find her. The police said if we didn't find the girl, I would be charged with shoplifting. Of course, we didn't find the girl because I was lying. The police took me back to the store so the manager could identify me. When the manager saw me, he identified me as the person he had seen running out of the store.

The policemen took me to the county jail. After they had taken all my personal information, they asked me if I wanted to call someone. I told them no because I knew there wasn't anyone I could call who would come and bail me out of jail. A police officer took me to a jail cell and locked me in. The jail cell had a sink, a toilet, and a bed with a thin mattress that was very uncomfortable to sleep on.

As I sat in the jail cell a bail bondsman came to the cell and asked me did I have any money to bail myself out. I said, "No", then he asked me did I have anybody I could call who would put up the money to bail me out. I told him, "No". He gave me his card and told me if I came up with some money I could give him a call. I didn't pay him any mind because I knew there was no one I could call that I could get money from. I figured I did the crime so I had to do the time.

I sat in the county jail for six to seven hours. Then I was taken to prison, where I had to stay until I received a court date.

Being in jail was the worst experience of my life. I became claustrophobic from being closed in. I started hyperventilating. I couldn't sleep. I was told when to eat, when to shower, and the food was nasty. There were people in jail from all different backgrounds, and some of the women looked and acted like men.

The lady with whom I shared a cell told me that when I got out, I shouldn't do anything that would cause me to ever get locked up again because I wasn't a person who could adjust to prison life.

The only good thing that went on in jail was the church services I attended on Wednesday nights. The only reason I went to the services was that I didn't have anything else to do, and I knew that I needed God's help to get me out of jail. I promised God that if He got me out of jail, I would never do anything else that would cause me to get locked up again, and I meant it from the bottom of my heart.

After two days of being locked up, I decided that I would try to call someone, but when I went to the phone to dial a number, I couldn't remember anyone's phone number.

After being locked up for four days and five nights, a few other girls and I were finally scheduled to appear before the judge. We were told to put all of our belongings into a bag because we didn't know if we were going to be released or not. We had to wait in our cells until our names were called. I was so anxious, and it seemed like it took forever for them to call my name.

We were transported in a prison paddy wagon. In the back of the wagon, there were two benches, one on each side, with a gate in between to separate the prisoners. The space between the gate and the benches was very narrow. About five ladies were cramped on each side, and everyone's hands were handcuffed behind them. It was a very hot day, and there were no windows in the back of the paddy wagon where we were.

After arriving at the courthouse, we were put in holding cells until our names were called for us to appear before the judge. We couldn't see each other, but we could talk to one another. We weren't supposed to have cigarettes or matches in our possession, but some of us managed to slip them into the cell. When we wanted to smoke, we would pass each other a cigarette and a match, take a couple of puffs from the cigarette, and then put it out.

When court started, the judge began taking the prisoners first. Everyone who was seen by the judge before me was sentenced to go back to jail, and I thought the judge was going to send me also. But when I went before him, he released me with time served. I was the happiest person walking. Even though I had a long walk home, I didn't care, just as long as I was out of jail.

I hadn't gotten high for five days. A person would think that after what I went through, I shouldn't want to get high, especially with the drugs out of my system, but as soon as I was released, the only thing I could think about was getting high. I started walking toward Remsen Avenue, where all the drug dealers and drug addicts hung out.

On my way to Remsen Ave., I saw this man who had a crush on me driving by in his car and I flagged him down because I wanted him to buy me some drugs.

After he picked me up, we rode around and talked. I started telling him about my jail experience. As time went on, I asked him if he could buy me some drugs. He tried to talk me out of getting high, but I didn't want to hear what he was saying. All I wanted to do was get high, so I made him a proposition. I told him that if he bought me some drugs, I would have sex with him. I knew he wasn't going to turn me down because for a long time he had been trying to get me into bed, but every time he would suggest having sex with me I would make up an excuse not to.

We went to the projects, brought the drugs, and went to my apartment to have sex. Even though I didn't like anything about him, I pretended to enjoy the sex because I didn't want him to know just how much I hated having sex with him. He was a nice person, but he was nasty-looking to me. I didn't want to have sex with him, but I wanted to get high just that badly. While we were having sex, the condom broke. I didn't like that at all because if I didn't like a person, I didn't want their bodily fluids in me. I jumped up and ran to the bathroom so I could hurry up and clean myself. After he had finished cleaning himself up, I rushed him out of my apartment so I could get high while I looked over my mail that had sat in the mailbox while I was locked up.

It was about five-thirty in the morning when I ran out of cocaine and when my heroin high had worn off. I wanted more, so I decided to go outside to look for either someone who was looking for someone to get high with or a man looking to trade money for sex. No one stopped to pick me up, but as I was walking, I found a five-dollar bill lying on the side of the curb. It wasn't enough to buy any drugs with, so I went back home and went to bed. I always thought that God was looking out for me when I found money or came upon drugs without having to have sex, but now I realize it was the devil allowing me to find money to try to keep me strung out on drugs.

INTO
HIS MARVELOUS
LIGHT

My Rehabilitation Process

Even though I continued to get high, the spirit of God was still drawing me. One Saturday, I got high all day and all night. By Sunday morning, I was tired. I felt, looked, and smelled bad, but I still had a strong desire to go to church. I decided to go to Pastor Bellamy's church. I didn't care about my physical appearance or how I smelled; all I wanted was for God to deliver me from my addiction so I would be able to function without drugs.

When Pastor Bellamy made a plea for the unsaved to get saved, I ran up to the altar. She laid hands on me and prayed for me. Each time I went to church, I would go up for prayer because I knew I wasn't delivered yet, and I desperately wanted to be delivered from drugs. Every time Pastor Bellamy laid hands on me and prayed, the strongholds that the devil had on me were broken.

I attended Pastor Bellamy's last crusade tent service that was scheduled for the year. A guest speaker from Trenton, N.J., Evangelist Tracey Troy, was the speaker for the night. After the service, my mother took me over to her as she approached her car. My mother told her I was scheduled to go to rehab and asked her if she would pray for me.

As we were standing on the side of the road, the evangelist from Trenton laid hands on me and prayed. After she was done, she looked me straight in the eye and told me, "When you go back to rehab this time, you will not have a desire to use drugs anymore." My mother understood more about prophecy and believed more than I did because she was saved and I wasn't, so she began praising God right there on the side of the road. Even though I continued to use drugs, God was working in my life, turning things around even though I didn't realize it at the time.

My sister introduced me to a drug dealer. I had only known him for about a month. The day before I was to get picked up for rehab, I called him because I wanted to buy some cocaine. After buying a ten-dollar bag of cocaine from him, I began telling him I was going into a rehabilitation facility the following morning. I also told him I was tired of getting high and that I wanted to stop using drugs so I could live a better life. He told me I was making a good decision, gave me back my ten dollars, wrote down his telephone number, and handed it to me. He told me that if I needed anything, I should give him a call, and he would help me out any way he could. I didn't take him seriously because I felt like most drug dealers don't want people who are using drugs to stop using because that's less money for them. Even though I felt this way, I put his number in my pocket.

That night, I packed my belongings in between taking hits of cocaine. It took me all night to smoke my ten-dollar bag. By seven-thirty, all of my things were packed, and I only had one hit of cocaine left. I finished my last hit as the van driver knocked on the door. When I opened the door to let him in, I was very paranoid, and I knew he could tell I was high by the way I acted and the way my eyes looked. I figured from his experience of transporting addicts to and from rehab, he must have known, but he helped me put my luggage into the van and never said anything about it to me as we drove off to the facility.

As he drove, we began talking, and I found out that he was a Christian man. I began telling him about my Christian grandmother and how she had raised me, teaching my siblings and me about God. I told him I was in this situation because I didn't listen to my grandmother and how I now wished I had. I was tired of using drugs. He was very attentive, understanding, and patient with me.

The rehab facility was about thirty minutes away from my house, but the ride seemed longer because I was high and paranoid. After arriving and completing some paperwork, the driver took me to a motel where I would be living during my stay.

The rehabilitation center rented several rooms from a motel owner on Route 22 for everyone who was in the rehabilitation program to live in while they were in treatment. The men weren't allowed in the women's rooms, and the women weren't allowed in the men's rooms. Three people were assigned to a room, and each person was responsible for paying thirty dollars a week for room and board. We had to supply our own food, wash our own clothes, and buy our own personal items. My mother was getting my welfare check so she could take care of my children and pay the bills at my apartment, and she agreed to pay for my room and board at the rehabilitation facility, but I was responsible for providing everything else I needed. I had no money, so that would be a problem for me.

In times past, after being at a rehabilitation facility for a few days, I would begin to regret making the decision to rehab, but this time was different; I really wanted to be there. It was the strangest thing: after stepping foot on the rehab property, I had no desire to use drugs anymore, just like the visiting speaker told me. It wasn't because I couldn't get any drugs either, because there were people in rehab who still managed to get some drugs. As a matter of fact, one of the counselors at the facility would bring drugs to the motel so she and a couple of the other girls could get high. Eventually, the counselor and the other girls got caught using drugs on the property. The counselor was fired, and the other ladies were put out of the program.

I would pray while I was taking a shower because this was the only private place I could find to spend time talking to God. I would pray so long and loud that the girls walking past my room would hear me. The girls began picking on me for praying, but I didn't care because I wanted God to protect and keep me from using drugs while I was in rehab. And He did just that.

I remember calling my mother one evening. This evening seemed different from any other day because when I looked up at the sky as I was talking to my mother, I noticed the sky was so beautiful. I was so excited that I stopped talking in the middle of my conversation with my mother just to tell her how beautiful the sky was. This was the first time in thirty years of my life that I had noticed how beautiful the sky was. I had been drug free before for up to thirty days, but this was the first time I realized and noticed the beauty in things and people.

After moving into another room on the other side of the motel, I began dating a guy who was also in the program. Everyone thought he was crazy, but I believed he was just acting crazy to get a disability check, so I started dating him because he had money and was willing to buy me the things I needed and wanted.

When the other women at the facility found out he was buying me things, they got jealous and told the counselors I was dating the guy and that he was buying me things. We weren't allowed to date anyone in the facility, so the staff members told us to stay away from each other. I didn't want to get in trouble, so I decided not to see him anymore. He didn't want to stop seeing me, so he began harassing me by trying to scare me into dating him again. He tried to make me believe that if I didn't date him, something was going to happen to me. He would try to intimidate me by placing a chair right outside my room. He would sit in it for long periods of time and try to watch my every move. He would also send me gifts, and if I didn't respond to them, he would threaten me. He kept doing this until, finally, I gave in to him and started dating him again. Even though I continued dating him, I stopped letting him buy me groceries because I started feeling bad about using him. I was not in love with him, but I continued to date him because I was scared of what he might do to me if I didn't.

I didn't have anyone I could go to for help when I needed food or personal items. I remembered the drug dealer who had given me his number, so I decided to call him. I told him I had to buy my own food and personal hygiene items, and I also had to wash my own clothes, but I didn't have any money to do it with. He asked me for the address where I was so he and his girlfriend could bring me some money. I gave it to him. A couple of days later, he and his girlfriend brought me some groceries, gave me money to wash my clothes and for other items that I needed.

Not once did he mention drugs to me. The only thing he said to me was, "If you need anything else, please don't hesitate to give me a call." He also told me I looked good and to keep up the good work. After showing him around the motel and explaining to him what was required of me, he and his girlfriend left.

I had to call him one other time because I needed him to go to my house for me and pick up some more clothes and shoes. He didn't hesitate to do it for me. He just went to my apartment, picked up the items I needed, and brought them to me.

I'm a person who always tries to repay those who help me or lend me money, so I told him that when I came home, I would repay him for everything he did for me. He never responded to what I said; he just gave me a hug and left.

During one of my counseling sessions, I told my counselor about not being able to buy food, clothes, and other items that I needed, and about the drug dealer who had helped me. My counselor didn't like the idea of me having dealings with a drug dealer; neither did she like the fact that he was on the premises, so she forbade me from seeing him again. She didn't think it was a good idea for me to have any type of dealings with a drug dealer because she was afraid he would try to sell me or other patients drugs, and she also felt he would expect me to pay him back by selling drugs for him when I was released from rehab. Even though I felt in my heart that her suspicions were false, I obeyed her, and I never called him again while I was in the rehabilitation facility.

The girls in rehab began to do devious things to me because they were jealous and envious of me. I couldn't understand why they felt this way because I was very nice to them. Looking back, I realize now that it was the enemy using them because of the mercy and favor of God upon my life. The girls tried their best to get me to take part in the wrong activities they were doing, but I couldn't because the Spirit of God was convicting and drawing me.

Since I was HIV positive, it was mandatory that I attend an HIV/AIDS support group that was held in a church building every Wednesday night. Most of the people who attended the meetings were very sick and frail-looking, except for me. As a matter of fact, had I never told anyone I had the virus, no one would have known. Some of the people who found out didn't believe I had the virus. They thought I was telling a lie. They said I looked healthy to them.

At the meetings, I always talked about the goodness of the Lord and how He was working in my life. God had become so real to me that I began telling people in the group that it was God who was keeping me healthy.

Because of his sickness and the way he was suffering, a guy who was in my group refused to believe in God. He said, "If God was so good and loving, how could He allow people to get an incurable disease like AIDS?" I told him, "The wages of sin are death, and because of the bad, sinful choices we made, it caused us to contract the disease, not God!"

After going to the meeting, I found out that a lady I knew from my home also attended the meetings. We would always talk and encourage one another. She would always bring her children with her to the meetings, and someone would watch them while she attended the meeting. I couldn't bring my children because I was in a rehabilitation facility, and my children were too far away for me to bring them, but I knew once I got out of rehab, I could bring my children with me as well.

The HIV support group leaders tried to make sure we were stress-free, and in doing so, people would donate items we needed, such as food or clothing, and give us the items we required. I didn't have very many clothes, and I had no money to buy any, so I always took clothes. I would take the clothes back to my motel room, and as soon as I put them in my room, my roommates would steal them. I knew one of my roommates was stealing from me, but I wouldn't say anything to her because I didn't want to have a confrontation with her. I wasn't scared of the girls; God was changing me, and I wanted to keep the peace. Wanting to keep the peace by not saying anything didn't help because my two roommates felt I was scared. One of my roommates went even further and tried to start a fight with me for no reason. No matter how she tried, I would not fight her because God helped me realize it was the devil using her. Instead of fighting her, I put in a request for a room change. On the request form, I explained why I wanted a room change. The administrator of the lodging facility tried to get me to change my mind, but I wouldn't because I was fed up with my roommate's actions.

After the administrator realized I was not going to change my mind about moving, she changed my room. I was placed in a room on the other side of the hotel, over the guy with whom I was having a relationship. My new roommate was dealing with her past. She oftentimes spoke of committing suicide. I would talk to her and try to make her feel better.

After I moved into my new room, it wasn't long before I began praying while I took showers. I would get in the shower, and while the water ran down my body, I would pray. I would pray loud and long for at least an hour at a time. I prayed as if I were saved, and saved for a long time. I would pray so loudly that the women would hear me as they walked by my room. A few of the women made it known that they heard me praying and asked me to pray for them also.

I stayed to myself most of the time. I never had many friends, so this was not strange for me. I considered myself a loner. The only person I would hang out with was the guy with whom I had a sexual relationship. I would sneak into his room and have sex with him, then sneak back out. Sneaking into his room was easy because I had no friends at the rehabilitation facility, and neither did he, so we weren't missed if no one saw us for a while. As I was coming out of his room one day, someone happened to see me. They told one of the counselors at the motel, and then the counselor told the administrators. When Monday morning came, we were both asked to report to the office. As a result of not obeying the rules of the facility, we were both asked to leave. The head of the administration told me that because I was court-ordered to attend a rehabilitation facility, I had to choose another one or I would not get my children back. I couldn't imagine having to go to another rehabilitation facility to start over. I had already done a month at the facility I was in. I didn't want to stay in rehab any longer than I already had. I refused to go to another in-patient facility. When I went back to the motel, I called my aunt to come pick me up. I packed my things, left the facility that night, and went home. After arriving home, to my surprise, I found out that my mother had given away her box spring mattress and had put her top mattress on top of my mattress in my room. All of my things were gone from my room, and she had put all of her things in my room. I had to sleep on a twin-sized bed in my living room. I didn't like these living arrangements, but I felt that my mother had the upper hand because she had custody of my children, so I dealt with the situation.

I had to wait a couple of weeks before I could get into an out-patient program. Even though the DYFS wanted me in an in-patient program, they agreed to let me go to an out-patient program as long as I had random drug testing. I also had to attend the program until I was released.

God was still working in my life, and I began to feel bad about having sex with guys. I wanted these guys out of my life for good, so I figured if I told them that I was HIV positive, they wouldn't want to see me again. I told them that while I was in rehab, I was tested for the AIDS virus, and it came back positive. I told them that they should get tested. None of the men got mad; they just thanked me for being honest and for telling them about having the virus.

One of the guys I told didn't believe me because he said I didn't look like I had the virus. I had to prove to him that I was HIV positive by showing him my HIV medications that I was on. Even though I showed him proof he still insisted on spending the night and having sex with me. I could tell that it bothered him that I was HIV positive and I also felt that he was undecided if he wanted to continue to see me or not. He told me that he had been seeing someone else and she was pregnant by him. He expressed to me that he didn't know how he was going to tell her he was sleeping with someone that was HIV positive. I told him that she had a right to know so she could get checked. The next morning he left and I didn't see him again for a long time. All the guys that were tested were negative, but they were told that they should continue to get tested every six months.

The next day, after my friend left, my mother came into the living room ranting and raving about me having an overnight male guest. She told me that she wasn't going to have men staying overnight. I told her that this was my apartment and I could have whomever I wanted over to my apartment for as long as I wanted them to stay. My mother had taken over my apartment, and it made me very angry, but I felt like I couldn't do anything about it because she still had custody of my children.

As I was going through my belongings, I came across the drug dealers' phone number who had helped me while I was in rehab, so I decided to give him a call. I wanted to repay him for all he had done for me while I was in rehab. When I got in touch with him I told him that I wanted to repay him for helping me, but to my surprise he told me that I didn't owe him anything. He told me to just keep up the good work and to stay clean. I thanked him and that was the last time I heard from him.

A couple of weeks had passed, and it was time for me to start my rehabilitation program. A van would pick me up and bring me home. I had attended this same program in the past, but I didn't take my recovery seriously. This time, I wanted to stay clean, so I had made up my mind to take the program seriously and to participate fully. In the meetings, I was very talkative; I made sure I talked about how I felt because I had a lot of hurt inside me and many problems I had to deal with. The first thing I needed to deal with was my living arrangement with my mother. I felt like a boarder in my own apartment. I always felt very uncomfortable living with someone else. I had promised God that if He blessed me with my own apartment, I would never live with anyone else if I could help it. Up until this point, I had kept that promise. I explained to my counselor what I was going through at home and how it made me feel. He told me that I should thank my mother for helping me keep my apartment and for taking care of my children while I got the help I needed. Then he said I should let my mother know in a nice way how I felt about her sleeping in my room and me sleeping in the living room since the apartment was mine. I took my counselor's advice and explained to my mother how I felt, but my mother didn't want to hear what I had to say. She got very upset and started an argument with me because she did not want to give me my room back. After several days of not speaking to each other, I decided to apologize to my mother for raising my voice at her. Then I calmly reminded her of our agreement prior to my going to rehab. I told her that I had asked her not to bother my room and that she could make the living room her bedroom. My mother realized that she was wrong and agreed to give me back my room. The next day, when I came home from the outpatient rehab clinic, my mother had put all of her things in the living room and all of my things into the bedroom. Coming home and finding the rooms switched around made me very happy. I could now have the privacy that I wanted, and by getting my privacy back, I also felt as though I was gaining control of my apartment.

Once I Was Blind But Now I Can See!

My mother had custody of my children while I focused on my rehabilitation. I continued to go to the outpatient program and attend Narcotics Anonymous meetings at least five to six times per week. I also went to HIV/AIDS support group meetings that were held once a week, but there was still something missing in my life, so I decided to attend church services with my mother and my children.

Pastor Elois Bellamy of Deliverance Prayer Revival Tabernacle is an anointed woman of God. She prayed the prayer of faith, and God delivered me from drugs. Even though God had taken the desire to use drugs away, there were other things I needed to be delivered from, so every time the Spirit of God would tell me to go up to the altar for prayer, I would go.

Pastor Bellamy would pray the prayer of faith over me, and I was slain in the Spirit by the power of God. When I got up off the floor that night, I was not the same. I remember being helped off the floor and placed on the front pew. As I began to look around, the Spirit of God opened my blinded eyes. The experience of God opening my eyes felt as if I had duct tape over my eyes and someone came by and snatched it off.

Experiencing this helped me to understand the true meaning of Isaiah 35:5which readsThen the eyes of the blind shall be opened, and the ears of the deaf shall be unstopped (NKJ).I was not the same after this experience. I wanted more of God than I wanted anything else, so I began praying and reading my bible and trying to understand the word of God even more.

When I read the word of God, I couldn't understand it, even though I was raised in church and was taught to read my Bible every day. As I read the word, I would get frustrated and put the Bible down. I had a deep hunger to know God, and I wanted to understand His word, so I would pick the Bible back up and begin reading again. Still not understanding what I was reading, I would get frustrated again. I did this until one day the Spirit of God led me to pray about the situation.

I told God this was His word and He left it here for us to live by, so I needed to understand what I was reading. Then I asked God to help me understand His word. As I continued to read the scriptures, God began to open up my understanding. I began to understand God's word as I read, and God began to give me revelation and knowledge of His word. Praise God! All wisdom, knowledge, and understanding come from God. God is my teacher!

Even though God had saved me, opened up my eyes, and helped me to understand His word, I still had a problem with smoking cigarettes. I realized that the Spirit of God could not dwell in an unclean body, so I knew I had to stop smoking! I made many attempts to stop smoking. I tried everything I could think of.

I never liked asking people for cigarettes, so I was okay not buying them, thinking that if I didn't have any, I would stop.

That didn't last long because as soon as the cravings came and I couldn't take it anymore, I would either ask the lady who lived upstairs from me for cigarettes. Again, I was back to square one because I didn't like begging for cigarettes; I would buy some.

I tried breaking cigarettes in half and smoking half of a cigarette. Then, I would take the other half of the cigarette and put it in the Newport box. I thought if I did this, I would smoke less, but this didn't work either. I tried keeping the cigarettes, using my willpower not to smoke them; this didn't work either.

I desperately wanted to stop smoking, so I figured if I talked to Pastor Bellamy about it, maybe she could help me. After church service one Sunday, I went up to her and told her about my cigarette problem. She responded by telling me, "You've got to make an effort." I thought I had already done all I could do to stop smoking. Finally, God spoke to me and told me to pray to Him for help. I walked home fast that night because all I could think about was getting home to get rid of the pack of cigarettes I had and to fall on my knees and pray. After returning home, I took all the cigarettes that were in the cigarette box and gave them to the lady who lived upstairs. Then I took the cigarettes I had broken in half, crushed them up, and put them in the garbage. I got down on my knees and I prayed.

I told God, "I realize Your Spirit cannot dwell in an unclean body, so I have tried everything I can think of to stop smoking, but nothing has worked." I confessed to God, "I can't stop smoking by myself, and I need Your help. Please, God, take the taste for cigarettes away from me." I thanked Him, then I went to bed. When I got up the next morning, my nightgown was soaking wet. I didn't know why it was wet, but I didn't smoke a cigarette all that day.

The next morning, when I got up my nightclothes were

wet again, but they weren't as wet as the night before. I became a little puzzled, so I mentioned it to my mother. My mother knew why my clothes were wet every morning. She said, "God is delivering you from those cigarettes."

On the second day, after praying, I went without smoking a cigarette, and I didn't have a desire for one. The third morning, I woke up; my clothes were a little wet but not as wet as the morning before. I didn't smoke a cigarette that day either. God had taken the taste of cigarettes away and cleaned the nicotine out of my body. I haven't smoked a cigarette since. Praise God!

I continued to spend my daytime hours at the out-patient drug rehabilitation clinic. Some days, I would attend group meetings, and once a week, I would meet with my counselor for a one-on-one counseling session. He needed to determine how my rehabilitation process was coming along, and he wanted to make sure I was doing everything that the rehabilitation facility expected of me for my recovery.

I did everything that was required of me. I attended the program every day. I participated in the program by going to all the meetings and being active during the meetings. My counselor said that he saw a change in me. He also felt that it was time for me to get on with my life.

I completed my six months in the out-patient program successfully; I was given a certificate of completion. I didn't have to attend the program anymore, but it was recommended that I attend a Narcotics Anonymous meeting at least three to four times a week.

God delivered me from drugs and cigarettes, and I didn't curse anymore. God delivered me from cursing without me asking Him. I was very excited about being saved because I was not spiritually dead anymore. (All things had passed away, and all things became new). I would always argue, fuss, and fight, but when God changed me, I didn't want to anymore. I wanted to be in a peaceful environment.

When God cleansed me I stopped dropping by friends home to sit around drinking and smoking. The desire to hang out at the bars was gone. I changed people, places and the things I did, but I soon realized those new acquaintances that were at the N.A and A.A meetings no longer drank alcohol or used drugs, but they were addicted to other things that I no longer participated in. This helped me to understand the need to become more focused on spiritual things and draw closer to God.

An old acquaintance came by my apartment because he wanted me to hang out and party. I told him that I was saved and I didn't do that anymore. I told him the only thing we could do together was go to church. He didn't like that idea, so he left and I never saw him again. I continued to attend church at Deliverance Prayer Revival Tabernacle as I grew in God. Each time I went to church to praise the Lord God, He would do something for me spiritually. I became stronger and stronger in the Lord.

I had given my life to the Lord, and it was time for me to be baptized. A lady went around the church, taking the names of the people who wanted to be baptized. I had my name put on the list for the next baptism.

Pastor Bellamy also made an invitation for all those who wanted to join the church to come forward. The Spirit of God began to deal with me concerning the ministry. Some people who belonged to the church were doing things that seemed "worldly" to me.

It was not long before I realized that God didn't want me to join this particular church. There was a tug-of-war going on between my flesh and the Spirit of God. The Lord kept telling me not to join the church, and I didn't want to leave because

Pastor Bellamy had interceded to God so earnestly for my deliverance. I couldn't understand why God didn't want me to join this church, but out of obedience, I did not join, and I began looking for another church to attend.

The following Sunday, I went to another church. Again, when the altar call was made, I went up for prayer. I knew I was saved and delivered from drugs, but I felt I still needed prayer. I needed God to change my old way of thinking and the way I reacted to certain things. I also wanted God to help me make godly decisions about several issues I had to deal with, and I wanted Him to continue strengthening me so I could stay saved and delivered.

As I stood at the altar along with several others, I began to feel the presence of the Lord, which caused me to weep. When the pastor finished praying the sinner's prayer with us, he then asked who wanted to join the church. I made the decision to join the church. I thought that because I had felt the presence of the Lord, this would be a good church to join. Everyone who made the decision to join the church was led to the back and placed in a room where we were given forms to fill out. As I began to fill out the form, I heard the Lord tell me not to join. Immediately, I got the attention of the man who was in charge, and I told him I could not join and why. He was very understanding.

The following Sunday, I decided to go back to Deliverance Prayer Revival Tabernacle Church. After the service, I went up to Pastor Bellamy. After I had greeted her, she said, "I missed you last Sunday, daughter. Where were you?" I began to tell her that I had visited another church because I was looking for a church home. She replied by telling me I should join the church where I got saved and delivered. I had to be honest with her because I knew what God had told me. I felt bad about having to tell her I couldn't join her church, but I had to obey

God. At that time, I didn't understand why God didn't want me to join her church, but now I do. I'll explain why a little later.

I left the church that day frustrated and a bit angry because I needed a church home and I didn't know where to go. I decided to pray and ask God what church He wanted me to join. When I prayed, I reminded God that He told me not to join the church where I was saved, and neither did He want me to join the other church I visited. I expressed to God that I really needed a church home and I needed Him to tell me what church family He wanted me to belong to. I remember being so angry that I banged my fist on the bed as I talked to him. God spoke to me that night and told me to go to the church that a friend of mine had told me about when she and I attended HIV/AIDS group meetings.

My cousins belonged to the church, so as soon as I finished praying, I called my cousin-in-law and told her that God wanted me to come to her church. I also told her that I would need a ride to church. My cousin-in-law was very happy that God had delivered me from drugs and that I had given my life to Him, so she said she would be more than happy to pick me up for church. The following Sunday, my cousin, his wife, and their three children came by for me.

God told me to go to this church, so when I went, I went with all intentions of staying. I had a good time praising the Lord. I was so excited about being saved and delivered from drugs, but I knew I needed to be baptized.

When church was over, I went to my cousin-in-law and told her that I wanted to be baptized. She told me I needed to talk to the pastor. She took me to Pastor Glenford Brown of New Creation of the Apostolic Faith and told him that I needed to talk to him. He took me to the back to the dining area of the church so we could have privacy, and I began to tell him how I was on drugs and how God delivered me and that God told me to come to this church. I also told him that I wanted to get baptized. We also talked about another church to which we both had belonged prior to that time. Before our talk ended, the pastor told me to keep coming to service and to keep praising the Lord.

I did as he told me to do. I kept coming to church. I attended Bible study, prayer meeting, Sunday morning, and evening services. I never missed a service if I could help it because I loved and appreciated God for taking me out of darkness and bringing me into His marvelous light.

Before each service ended, everyone was asked to come around the altar for a congregational prayer. I always prayed to God from my heart. Tears continually flowed from my eyes because I loved and appreciated God. God is an awesome and mighty God. Only God could deliver me from seventeen years of misery and strife, heartache and pain, a life filled with drug use, low self-esteem, lying, stealing, and prostitution. All I could do was thank God and dedicate my life to serving Him.

As I attended our scheduled church services, Pastor Brown would watch me. I didn't know why at the time, but I believed in my heart he wanted to make sure that I was serious about my salvation and to see how God was moving in my life.

My son's godmother had donated some clothes to the Salvation Army, and somehow the clothes ended up at the outpatient rehabilitation clinic that I went to. I had chosen all of her clothing. I didn't know they were her clothes until I got home and showed my mother the clothes. My mother said those clothes looked just like the clothes my son's godmother owned. After talking to my son's godmother, we realized that they were her clothes.

I was getting dressed to go to a NA meeting. I picked out one of the sweat suits that I had gotten from the goodwill box at the rehabilitation clinic to wear. After I had put the pants on, I heard the voice of the Lord tell me to take off the pants. When God speaks, you will hear and know it's His voice. I didn't have a clothes closet in my room, so I had to use a clothes rack to hang my clothes on. I took off the pants, then I stood up on my bed and faced the clothes rack. I began to talk to the Lord. I said, "Okay, God, you told me to take off the pants and I don't have any dresses to wear so I need you to provide me with some dresses to wear." After I finished talking to the Lord I found an old jean skirt that I had, I put it on and went to the NA meeting.

It didn't take God long to provide me with the dresses, skirts and suits that I needed. People I didn't even know began giving me clothes. Not only did my son's godmother give me a hundred and fifty dollar suit with the price tag still on it, I had more than I could have imagined. I had so many clothes that I didn't have enough room to fit them on the clothes rack.

As I continued to attend the Narcotics Anonymous group meetings, God began to minister to me about the things I confessed each time I went to a meeting. He told me that each time I said, "Hi, my name is Arlene, and I am an addict," I was confessing to be a drug addict. After God opened up my understanding to this fact, I made up my mind I wasn't going to say I was an addict anymore. I wanted to say I was delivered, but I knew if I used the word delivered people at NA meeting wouldn't understand what I was talking about, so I decided to say I was a recovered addict.

Members of Narcotics Anonymous believe that if someone is an addict, they will always be an addict, but they are either an active addict or an inactive recovering addict (meaning they are not using, but they are still an addict). That's why a person has to stand up and confess that they are an addict. If a person doesn't say he or she is an addict, people in NA will try to convince the person that they are in denial.

At the next meeting I attended, I stood up and said, "Hello, my name is Arlene, and I am a recovered addict." The room became very quiet. Everybody began looking around at one another. People couldn't wait until it was their turn to speak. They tried to convince me that I would always be an addict and that I shouldn't say I was recovered. They said I needed to take one day at a time in dealing with my recovery. I didn't pay them any attention because I knew God was the one who delivered me from drugs and he was able to keep me off of drugs.

When the meeting was over, I made up my mind never to attend another NA meeting again because I knew I didn't belong there. I decided to attend church services for encouragement and help with my spiritual growth and to totally trust God to keep me saved and drug-free.

I told you earlier that I would explain to you in more detail why God didn't want me to join the church where I got saved.

I need to say that the reason God didn't want me at Pastor Bellamy's church had nothing to do with the ministry or her leadership as a pastor.

Pastor Bellamy teaches "holiness or hell," and she has a very powerful deliverance ministry. She is an anointed woman of God who loves people from the depths of her heart. She loves seeing souls being saved and transformed by the power of God, and she loves doing the work of the Lord.

I need to say that a true ministry is birthed within, and you have to go through something in order to obtain true ministry and the anointing. God knows what His children need to experience to become effective witnesses for Him; He also knows what it's going to take to get them there.

"Let's take another look at my past for just a minute. I was on drugs for seventeen years, and I became a prostitute to get money to buy them."

The way I would get the money was by wearing tight jeans to entice men. I would put holes in my pant legs that went straight up to my bottom. Then I would walk up and down the street, switching my bottom to attract a man's attention.

Doing this became a way of life for me, so every time I put on a pair of jeans, I would act as if I were still trying to entice men. I would begin switching my bottom, and I thought I was "all that and a bag of chips." This way of thinking and behavior had to be changed. Therefore, I needed to be in an environment where pants were not allowed until my old way of thinking and behaviors changed.

Even though I obeyed God and didn't wear pants, I believe in my heart that if I were around other saved people who wore pants, I would have probably followed them and put the pants back on before God finished changing me.

I believe God was protecting me and preparing me for ministry. God knows that a person will, most of the time, do what other people do, and this is why He allowed me to grow under a strict apostolic ministry.

Being a member of New Creation Apostolic Church, I was taught to wear long skirts and dresses and not to wear pants, short skirts, or jewelry. I had to have my head covered while in the sanctuary and when I prayed.

I have learned since that viewing holiness as an outside appearance is wrong. I believe holiness comes from within. Some Christians put a lot of extra energy into judging people by what they wear. Don't get me wrong! I, myself, believe that a woman ought to dress modestly as unto God.

As I continued to worship God in the apostolic church, I wore my earrings because God didn't tell me to take them off, and neither did I see anything wrong with them.

One Sunday morning, I was at church, and the pastor's daughter came up to me and told me that I wasn't supposed to wear earrings. She said it is written in the Word that it is a shame for people to pierce their bodies. God had not revealed this to me, so I asked her where in the Bible this was found. She couldn't tell me, but out of obedience, I took them off.

There was another incident where I had worn a short-sleeved shirt to church, and another young female adult came up to me and told me that I shouldn't be wearing the shirt because it was "worldly." At the time, I had very few clothes to wear, so I got smart with the young lady. I told her if she didn't like what I had on, she should go and buy me another shirt. She didn't say anything else to me about what I wore.

I feel that Christians are to let God do His job. Too often, I find that they want to dress new converts before they are totally transformed by the power of God.

I believe that our job as Christians is to pray for one another, let the pastor and all those who are anointed to preach the word, and let God do the convicting and changing.

When Christians tell a new Christian what to wear and what not to wear, they are trying to do God's job. As a result, the new Christian will sometimes become offended or end up putting back on whatever they were told to take off. However, when God cleans a Christian up on the inside, it will show on the outside. The person does not become offended, and he or she won't revert back because it is settled in his or her heart.

From experience, I've found that if a person goes to a church wearing jewelry, pants, a skirt, or a dress just above the knee, and if that particular church does not believe she should be dressed this way, the people at the church automatically believe the person is not "saved."

I, on the other hand, believe that a Christian should righteously judge a person by the fruits they bear. I've seen people who wear long skirts, who don't wear jewelry, and have their heads covered, yet show no love toward me and others, and they would let the devil use them mightily as they bear fleshly fruits.

In my opinion, you can only measure or believe a person is a true Christian based on their behavior and whether they personify in their character the fruit of the spirit which is displayed in the form of love, peace, long-suffering, gentleness, goodness, faith, meekness, and temperance (Galatians 5:22-23). Unfortunately, there are Christians who judge their brothers and sisters by what they wear instead of the content of their character. Some people may not have anything else to wear except what they have on. God taught us how to dress. He is the same yesterday, today, and forevermore. He is powerful enough to do the same for anyone else whom He draws into His kingdom.

My Baptism, Holy Ghost, and Fire Infilling

I had to wait several months before Pastor Brown would baptize me. At the time, I couldn't understand why I had to wait so long, but I loved the Lord, and I wanted to do things right, so I waited patiently.

As the time drew near for me to be baptized, the Lord instructed me to go on a one-day fast and consecration. I obeyed the Lord and fasted on the day I was scheduled for baptism. I didn't eat or drink anything all that day.

As I stood in the water, all I could think about was that I was going to leave all the old "me" buried in the water. I went down in the name of Jesus, fasting and consecrated. I put on Christ; old things had passed away, and everything was new. There was no more trace of sin upon my life because I was buried in Christ. Hallelujah! To God be the glory; great things He has done for me!

Immediately after my baptism at Wednesday night Bible study, Pastor Brown began teaching about being filled with the Holy Ghost. As he taught, God began to open up my understanding of being filled with the Holy Ghost. Understanding it caused me to desperately want to be filled with the gift of the Holy Ghost, so I asked God to fill me.

On Friday nights, the church would have tarrying service. What happens on this night is that, at the end of the service, all those who wanted to pray or seek God for the infilling of the Holy Ghost would gather around the altar to do so. I was taught to call, "Jesus, Jesus, Jesus," until I was filled. I was at the altar seeking God for the Holy Ghost when a sister in the Lord came to pray with me. She was screaming in my ear so loudly that I couldn't concentrate. To avoid her screaming in my ear, I would go up and down, trying to get away from her, and then another sister in the Lord who didn't care for me very much came to tarry with me. When she put her hands on me, I immediately discerned her spirit, jumped up and went back to my seat. This was the last time I went to the altar to tarry for the Holy Ghost because I didn't want anyone tarrying with me. I made a decision that night: if I was going to be filled with the Holy Ghost, I was going to get filled seeking God alone.

The following Friday, I decided to stay in my bedroom, fasting and praying for the infilling of the Holy Ghost. As I prayed and fasted, I told God that He promised me the gift of the Holy Ghost, and I wanted to be filled. I told Him that at the next Friday night tarrying service, I wanted to be filled. I believe now that if I had asked God to fill me right there in my room, He would have filled me.At the next Friday night service I couldn't wait until tarrying service began. When my pastor started tarrying service, I ran to the front pew next to my pastor's wife. I knelt down and began to plead the blood of Jesus. On the third blood of Jesus the Spirit of God picked me up, twirled me around and laid me flat on my back on the floor. I began speaking in an unknown tongue as the Spirit of God gave me utterance. Pastor Brown came and stood over me to listen to me to see if I was really filled. I heard him clapping his hands and praising God as he listened to me speak in tongues. When prayer service was over he announced that God had filled me with the Holy Ghost. I was so excited! Out of my belly flowed living water. I didn't feel or act the same. I felt as if I was walking on a cloud. I rode the church van home that night and as I was getting out of the van to go into my apartment, Pastor Brown told me to enjoy the Holy Ghost. I didn't understand in depth what he was talking about at the time, but I would soon find out. I was so excited and I couldn't wait to tell my mother I had gotten filled with the Holy Ghost. As soon as she opened the door to let me in my apartment I told her that I had gotten filled with the Holy Ghost. She hugged me and said, "Praise God!" She was very happy for me.When I returned home from church, it was rather late, so I prepared myself for bed. I got in the bed to go to sleep, but I could not sleep. I praised God for hours. When I finally fell asleep, I only slept for about one to two hours. I was up bright and early praising God as I cleaned the apartment. Every morning I would get up, pray and read my bible. I attended every scheduled church service because I loved praising God for what he had done for me, hearing the word because it helped me to grow. I also loved telling my testimony because I wanted others to know what God had done for me and what he continued to do for me.

Before God filled me with the Holy Ghost, I had the look of street life on me. If someone looked at me, they could tell that I had been out in the world for seventeen years. After God filled me with the Holy Ghost, I saw God perform a transformation in me.

I was looking in the mirror, and I noticed my face did not look the same. I looked at my hands, and they didn't either. My complexion had changed. It was lighter, and there was a glow about me. I looked as if I had never used drugs in my life.

The following Sunday, as I walked into the sanctuary, the devotional leader jumped when she saw me because she, too, noticed that my countenance had changed. Not only her, but my pastor also commented on my appearance. Before he got ready to preach, he asked me to stand up and face the congregation so they, too, could see the transformation God had made to my countenance.

Also, before the Lord filled me with the Holy Ghost, I would feel nervous around unsaved people or people with whom I used to get high. But after God filled me with the Holy Ghost, I didn't feel nervous anymore. I would tell them what God had done for me with boldness.

My mother still had custody of my children, while God continued to work on me. I thank God for my mother because I needed her to take care of my children so God could do what He needed to do in me.

I believe everything happens for a reason. As I look at how things turned out, I can say that it was a blessing that God allowed the Division of Youth and Family Services to take my children from me and give custody to my mother. God wanted me to be free of responsibilities so I could concentrate on Him and allow Him to do what He needed to do in me.

God had my undivided attention. I couldn't watch television because the Lord told me not to. For a year, I stayed by myself most of the time, fasting, praying, and reading my Bible. Each day, I grew stronger and stronger in the Lord as I continued to fast, pray, read my Bible, and attend scheduled church services.

God had given me what I was trying to find in drugs. He gave me joy, peace, contentment, a new walk, and a new talk. I had a different outlook on life; life was worth living.

When I was in the company of unsaved people who didn't have any respect for God or His children, I would have to leave because I couldn't take the swearing, their conversations, or the cigarette smoke.

When I went to the store or somewhere, I would run into an old acquaintance. We would start talking, and if they lit a cigarette, I would ask them if they could wait until we departed company because I couldn't stand the smoke. They would say, "Oh please! You used to smoke," and light it anyway. I would tell them, "God delivered me from cigarettes, and I can't take the smoke," and then I would leave.

When I went out somewhere and saw someone I knew, I would stop to speak to them. During our conversation, they would start using curse words. I would ask them nicely not to use those words around me. Some people would say, "Excuse me," when they slipped and said a curse word, but some of them didn't care and would continue to curse like there was no tomorrow.

My unsaved family members said I thought I was too good because I would not hang out with them, but that wasn't the case. God changed me. The things they did and talked about, I didn't engage in, so I couldn't be around them for long.

The thing I couldn't understand was that when I was a drug addict, they didn't want to be around me, but now that I was saved, I couldn't be around them. They couldn't call me a "crack head" anymore, but they would say I thought I was too good to be around them. When I began witnessing to them, they would say I was judging, and I couldn't tell them anything because I used to do the same things.

Before God filled me with the Holy Ghost, I was scared to go on Remsen Avenue to witness because I was afraid someone would try to talk me into using again. But after God filled me with the Holy Ghost, I wasn't afraid anymore. I would go there and witness. Old acquaintances would tell me how good I looked and how proud they were of me. I would tell them God delivered me, but some of them would say, "You had to want to be changed, or you had something to do with the change that took place in your life." They didn't want to give God the glory for changing me. I always let them know it wasn't anything I had done; it was all God's doing.

God Healed My Body Of A Deadly Disease

Although I was saved, delivered, and filled with the Holy Ghost, I still tested positive for the HIV virus. I had bleeding gums and a rash caused by the virus. I would go to my doctor's appointments once a month and take my medicine three times a day. I didn't want to die, so I decided to trust God for my healing.

Not only was my bedroom my secret closet, but the bathroom was too. I would take my worship music into the bathroom along with my CD player, run a tub full of water, and pour blessed oil in it. I would get in the tub and pray for hours at a time.

One night, as I was praying, the Spirit of God began making intercession for me. I began speaking in tongues, and then I started telling God that "He was wounded for my transgressions, He was bruised for my iniquities, and the chastisement of my peace was upon Him, and by His stripes I am healed." I began telling Him how He healed the blind man, raised the dead, and made the lame walk. I told God He was the same yesterday, today, and forevermore. Then I told God that I wanted Him to heal my body.

As I was praying, God told me to fast for five days. He said I couldn't eat or drink anything. When God gave me these instructions, I began weeping because I knew I had never fasted for such a long period of time before. I knew the only way I would be able to do it was if He helped me, so I told God that I was willing to fast, but I needed His help. I asked God to put the spirit of fasting in my spirit, in my desire, and in my determination. I prayed and thanked God for at least an hour.

When I got out of the tub, God had answered my prayer, and I started my five-day fast without food or water. I went on with my daily activities as I continued to fast, pray, and read the Word of God.

On the third day of the fast, God was leading me to drink water, but because God told me not to eat or drink anything, I thought it was the devil who was telling me to drink water, so I wouldn't drink any. I spoke to an evangelist at the church and explained to her what I was going through; she explained to me that I should drink water because I needed it after the third day. I took her advice and drank some.

The fourth day of my fast fell on the first Sunday, which was Communion Sunday. As I was getting ready for church, the devil told me that since I was taking communion, I would be breaking my fast anyway, so I could eat some food after church. At the time, I didn't know any better, so I made up my mind to eat after church, even though the Lord had told me not to eat for five days.

As we began the communion part of the service a spiritual war began between my flesh wanting to eat and obeying God. I went back and forth with God as the communion plate came closer to me. I got so aggravated that I told God if he didn't want me to break my fast to tell me something. The Spirit of

God spoke to me and said "I don't want you to eat or drink anything until after you take your blood test." My blood test was scheduled for the following day at five o'clock pm. When God mentioned my blood test, I knew that God really didn't want me to break my fast. I told God okay. As soon as I said okay, the communion plate came to me.

I didn't eat or drink anything until after I took my blood test the following day. After I took my blood test, I broke my fast with a lollipop that was given to me at the doctor's office.

I was scheduled to go back to see my doctor a month after I had taken my blood test. While I waited to see the doctor, I trusted God and believed He had healed my body, and I praised God for my healing every day.

The following month, I went to my doctor's appointment, and as I was sitting in the doctor's office talking to my doctor, the Lord spoke to me and told me to ask my doctor what my blood test results were. She looked at my blood work and started knocking on her wood desk as she said, "Your test is undetectable." As she knocked on the desk, I told her luck had nothing to do with it. It was God who had healed me. She went even further to say that there are other people who are undetectable but still have the virus. I didn't pay her any mind because I knew it was God who had healed my body.

I believe in my heart that not only would I have hindered my healing if I had broken my fast before the fifth day, but I would have been disobeying God while taking communion.

Even though I tested undetectable for the HIV virus, I continued to take my medicine and make all my doctor's appointments because my pastor told me that until God released me from taking my medicine, I should continue to take it prayerfully and go to my scheduled doctor's appointments.

The next thing I wanted God to heal me of was my

bleeding gums. Every time I brushed my teeth, my gums would bleed like crazy. I had some kind of gum disease, and it was very irritating and nasty to me. I remember standing in front of the bathroom mirror and asking God to heal my gums. A few days later, I realized my gums were not bleeding anymore when I brushed my teeth. God had healed my gums. Praise God! Jesus is my Savior, my deliverer, my friend, my provider, my joy, my peace, and my healer! As I continue to tell my life story you'll find that God proves himself to be everything I need.

After I became stronger in the Lord, I began witnessing to more people and telling them about Jesus and how He saved me, delivered me from drugs, and healed my body of the HIV virus.

I would always invite people to church. At first, they would turn down the invitation, but after praying and seeking God on their behalf, then going back and inviting them again, they would accept my invitation and come to church. My heart's desire was that they would give their lives to the Lord, but none of them did.

God Gave Me Back My Children

I dropped out of school in the ninth grade, and I hadn't worked for almost eleven years. It was suggested to me that I go back to school and learn a trade as part of my rehabilitation process. I had some typing training, so I decided to go to clerical school.

I was afraid of going back to school because I always had a problem with taking tests. I was a good student during the learning process, but when it was time for me to take tests, I would get so nervous that my mind would go blank, and I wouldn't remember the things I had learned. I would fail the test.

My mother had custody of my children; therefore, she was getting all of my public assistance money. My mother would make sure that I ate, but I had to purchase everything else that I needed. It was very hard for me at this time in my life because I had no job and no money. I began to seek God continuously about my schooling, my finances, and getting back custody of my children. I would pray day and night concerning these three things.

Before I started school, my mother invited me to attend a church service with her at her home church in Orange, NJ. During the service, my mother's pastor called me out and asked me to come to the altar. She prophesied to me and told me not to worry about my schooling and my finances. She said that God was going to supply my needs and see me through school. I knew God had revealed these things to her because I didn't tell anyone what I was going through, not even my mother. The only person I talked to about my situation was God. I was relieved to know that He had heard and answered my prayers yet another time.

The clerical school I signed up for was located in Edison, NJ. I had no transportation, so I had to walk from my house to downtown New Brunswick to the train station. The walk took about twenty-five to thirty minutes. After taking the train to Edison, a driver would meet me and several other people at the train station and then take us to the clerical school. I did this routine every day during the course of my clerical training.

I knew the only way that I was going to succeed in my clerical training was to lean and depend on God for help, so I prayed continually about my schooling. I always prayed before I left home in the morning, on the train, before tests, and after tests. God is a faithful God! When He said the Holy Ghost would bring all things back to my remembrance, He meant it. When I couldn't remember an answer to a question, I would bow my head and say a quick prayer, and as soon as I read the question again, God would bring the answer back to me. I learned to depend on God throughout the course of my clerical training.

A couple of weeks into my clerical training, I was scheduled to appear before the judge about getting custody back of my two children. I didn't see any reason why I shouldn't get them back because I had done all that was required of me. I was drug-free for six months. I had finished my outpatient rehabilitation treatment. I was doing my clerical rehabilitation training, and I was saved, sanctified, and filled with the Holy Ghost.

The judge I had to go before was very mean. His attitude caused me to feel nervous and intimidated. When I entered the courtroom, I was told to take a seat next to my public defender. A person from the Division of Youth and Family Services was seated at the other table along with their attorney.

Immediately after entering the courtroom, the judge said a few words, then gave the other side the floor to explain why they thought I shouldn't regain custody of my children. Then my lawyer stood and said a few words about my achievements. The judge stated that my children were to remain in the custody of my mother. When I replayed what had happened in the courtroom in my mind, I realized my lawyer wasn't fighting for me the way she should have. I felt like the odds were against me and that I was in a no win situation, but I didn't let the outcome get me down.

I was rescheduled to go back before the judge in a couple of months. In the meantime, I continued to do the positive things I was doing, along with praying and trusting in God.

When it came time for me to appear before the judge again, I was certain I would get my children back because of the progress I had made. During the ride to the courthouse, I expressed to the driver that I felt confident and sure I would leave court with custody of my children.

As I sat in the courtroom, I saw some unusual activity going on. A person came from the back and handed the judge a paper. The judge immediately ordered that my children remain in the custody of my mother, and he scheduled me to appear before him in another couple of months. I was so surprised and hurt by the judge's decision.

After court adjourned, my attorney told me a person from

the DYFS office faxed a letter to the judge telling him not to give me custody of my children because I had "beaten" my children and I wouldn't allow them to go outside to play on Sunday.

Immediately, I became furious with my mother because I knew she was the only one who could have given this information. She was the only one who knew I wouldn't allow my children to go outside to play on Sundays because I felt they needed a nap before we went back to evening service. My mother disagreed with me; she felt I should let them go outside to play. She was also the only one who had seen me spank my children at home. On the ride home from court, I thought my mother called DYFS because I felt she didn't want to give me back custody of my children. When I arrived home my mother said a person from DYFS called her to question her about how I handled my children in her presence. She told them about the two incidents.

I was so angry and hurt at my mother that I began yelling and screaming at her when I came home. I accused her of calling the DYFS. Even though my mother insisted a woman called her, I was still upset with her because, regardless of who called whom, I felt she shouldn't have told them what had happened. Her telling them what happened made me believe she didn't want me to get custody of my children. I was so angry with my mother that I wouldn't speak to her for a day or two.

God began dealing with me about the way I had spoken to my mother and about being mad at her. My conscience began to bother me, so I decided to forgive her and apologize to her for disrespecting her. While I waited a couple of months for my next court appearance, I continued to fast, pray, read God's Word, and trust Him to move on my behalf concerning my children even though the odds were against me.

I felt as if my lawyer was not fighting for me because she didn't speak up for me the way I thought she should. The judge was very rude and nasty toward me. The DYFS didn't want me to get custody of my children and I felt my mother wanted to keep custody of my children. I had no one on my side but God, so I prayed and trusted Him to move on my behalf.

On my third court appearance, God moved in a mighty way! To my surprise, God saw to it that I didn't have to stand before the judge who had been so nasty to me. God sent him on vacation and appointed another judge. God had prepared this judge's heart and mind to rule in my favor. To my surprise, as I entered the courtroom, the judge greeted me by saying, "Hello, Mrs. Branham! How are you?" I replied, "Hello, Your Honor."

The judge greeted me in such a loving, caring, and respectful way that it caused me to jump in shock when he addressed me, because I had never experienced this type of greeting from the other judge.

After the judge listened to the opening arguments from both sides, he boldly announced that no matter what the DYFS had to say, he had decided to give me back custody of my children.

The lady who represented the DYFS was upset about the judge's decision to give me back custody of my children so she asked to be heard. She wanted to reassure the judge of the reasons why he should reverse his decision. Again, the judge boldly told her he would hear what she had to say, but his decision was final.

When the woman from the DYFS spoke, she focused on my seventeen years of drug use. She felt that because of the length of time I had used drugs, she wanted to watch me a little longer before giving me back my children. She stated that most people who used drugs for such a long period of time usually went back to their drug use after some time. Before the prosecutor could sit down, my lawyer jumped up to defend me. It was as if a force lifted her from her chair. My lawyer never reacted like this for me in times past. All I could do was sit in amazement and watch God move on my behalf.

When both sides were done, the judge's decision still stood as he hit his gavel and made the final, binding announcement that I was to regain custody of my children.

As I look at the way things happened from the time I arrived at court until the time I regained custody of my children, I realize it was nobody but God who had moved on my behalf and given me back my children.

I had to tell what God had done for me. At the next Friday night service, I stood during testimony service to share what the good Lord had done for me.

A few weeks before my clerical training was up, I began looking for work in the clerical field. After searching and searching, I couldn't find a job. I wanted to work for the hospital as a unit clerk, so I filled out an application at Robert Wood Johnson Hospital for that position. I didn't type fast enough, so I wasn't able to get into the clerical field. I still wanted to work at the hospital, so I filled out an application for a position in housekeeping. I hadn't worked in a while because of my drug use, so getting a job seemed impossible due to my work history. I knew I had to pray and trust God to give me a job at the hospital.

I had to walk past the hospital every day to get to the train station, so every day as I walked past the hospital, I would claim a job in Jesus' name and praise God for it. I began speaking the job into existence. By the time my clerical training was over, the hospital called me for an interview. Everyone who came in for an interview had to take a test. I passed the test and got a job at the hospital in housekeeping. Praise God! God blessed me again. God continued to prove Himself to me over and over again.

I worked at the hospital for a year before getting hurt on the job. I suffered from two herniated discs in my upper and lower back and a pinched nerve. I was not able to work, but the hospital's doctor didn't think so. He gave me a neck brace and ordered me back to work. I was hurting so badly I couldn't even sit and be a patient monitor. I decided to get a lawyer and sue the hospital for my injuries.

My lawyer told me I had to go to work or they could fire me. He also told me that if I was unable to perform my duties, I should go to the employee's clinic at the hospital and let them send me home. Each day I went to work, I found that I couldn't perform my duties, so I did as my lawyer suggested. I went to the employee's doctor, and they would send me home. On payday, when I went to pick up my check, I was told I had to pick it up from my supervisor's office. Before my supervisor gave me my check, he told me I was fired. Hearing the news did not bother or upset me. I told him, "The same God who gave me this job would give me another one if He saw fit," and left the office.

When I went to apply for my unemployment benefits, the hospital tried to stop me from getting them because, if I was approved, by law the hospital was responsible for paying part of my unemployment benefits, and they didn't want to. They tried everything they could to stop me from getting my unemployment benefits, but nothing they tried worked because God was working on my behalf. Besides, who could fight against God and win? No one!

God Gives Me Favor with the Judge

Before I gave my life to the Lord, I got caught twice driving with no license. The first time I got caught, my license was revoked, even though I had never had a license before. The second time I got caught, I was charged with driving with a revoked license and a moving violation. When I was scheduled to go to court, I didn't show up, so I was charged with contempt of court.

I decided to take care of my fines so I could eventually be able to drive. When I went to court, the courtroom was full of people who had received tickets for moving violations, people who had been pulled over and didn't have a license, people who were involved in some kind of car accident, and people who didn't have car insurance.

My name was at the top of the list to be called because my last name begins with the letter B. When I stood before the judge, he read me my charges and asked me why I didn't show up in court when I was scheduled to come and why it took me so long to take care of this matter. I told him I had been on drugs for seventeen years and that all I cared about then was getting high. He then asked me if I was still using drugs. I told him I wasn't. He asked me how long I had been clean and sober, and I told him, "About two years." He congratulated me for being clean and sober for two years, then he asked me if I was working. I told him I was working at Robert Wood Johnson Hospital. The judge told me that with all the charges I was facing, I could get up to three thousand dollars in fines. Then he told me to have a seat, and he would get back to me.

I sat in the back of the courtroom until everybody else's cases were heard. Then the judge asked me why I was still there. I told him that he had told me to have a seat and that he would get back to my case. The judge told me to come back up before him, and as he read my fines, he dismissed all of them except one. When everything was said and done, I was only charged three hundred and some odd dollars. The judge told me to make sure I stayed on the road that I was on. I thanked the judge and left the courtroom. I was so happy! Instead of paying three thousand dollars in fines, all I had to pay was three hundred and some odd dollars. All I could do was give God all the glory, honor, and praise for giving me favor with the judge yet another time. When I went to the motor vehicle office, they told me I had to wait a year before I could get my license, but that was okay. Waiting a year would give me time to study for my written test.

At The Name Of Jesus Demons Have To Flee!

After my mother moved into her own apartment, I realized the apartment I lived in was too small. I didn't have a closet in my room. I kept my clothes in the hall closet, and it smelled of mildew. My kids' closet was too small for their things. They also needed separate rooms because they weren't the same sex.

I did most of my praying in the bathtub. I would pray for about an hour to two at a time. During my prayer time, I talked to the Lord and explained to Him how I needed a bigger apartment with more closet space and separate rooms for my children. Little did I know that God would move the lady who lived upstairs and move me up there. The landlord evicted the lady upstairs and offered me the apartment. I was not eligible for a four bedroom apartment, but the landlord fixed it so I could rent the apartment with access to the third floor also.

While the lady was moving out, the landlord came by the house to show me the upstairs apartment. He warned me that the apartment was very nasty. He said I wasn't going to believe my eyes. When I walked into the apartment, I couldn't believe my eyes. It was the nastiest place I had ever seen. It was as if she had never cleaned the apartment since moving in. Now I see why she wouldn't allow the exterminator into the apartment. She had piles and piles of dirty clothes all through the house. The white kitchen cabinets had food all over them. The refrigerator had dead roaches in the door. The stove looked like it was taken from a junkyard and never cleaned. The landlord and I agreed that he would have the apartment repainted, replace the carpet, the stove, and the range. In return, I would clean the apartment, and I wouldn't have to pay a security deposit.

When the painters came to paint the apartment, they were scared to go into the bedroom where the lady did her palm readings. The room had deer hooves, buttons, candles, beads, and it was full of demonic spirits. When I entered the room, I could feel the spirits. I had to pray and drive the demons out of the room. I thank God that at the name of Jesus, demons fear and tremble. Not only do they tremble; they have to flee.

After moving into the apartment, I still had to continue to go into that room and pray because the demons would come back and try to live. One day, I was praying through the house, and as I was praying, the Lord told me to go upstairs to the room where the lady did her palm readings and pray. As I proceeded to go up the stairs while I pleaded the blood of Jesus, demons attacked me. I felt like I had a ton of bricks on my back. I began to sweat. I fell to my knees going up the steps, pleading the blood of Jesus. I was determined to drive the demons out. I made it to the room where the demons were and cast them out of my apartment. Even after casting out the demons, God would lead me into his room to pray daily.

After the Lord blessed me with my four-bedroom apartment, I let a sister from our church come to live with me rent-free until she found a job. To earn her keep, she would cook, clean, and do laundry for me. After she got a job, she started paying rent.

I asked the landlord if this gentleman and his handicapped son could rent the downstairs apartment. I felt sorry for them because they lived in a rooming house where drug addicts hung out. This was the same gentleman who picked me up while walking home from the courthouse after I was let out of jail. He was also the same gentleman to whom I prostituted myself in exchange for some drugs.

The gentleman and his son were the two people who I didn't have to plead with to come to church. One reason was because he liked me and he was trying to do whatever he could to get me. He figured if he came to church and got saved I would date him. He figured wrong. Nothing about him interested me except for the fact he was a soul that needed to be saved.

Not only did I not want him; I knew the only reason he said the "sinner's prayer" was that he wanted me, and I wasn't going to marry anyone who got saved for me. I wanted a husband who wanted to serve God for himself.

Even though I was saved, I still had ways about me that were not right. I didn't like the gentleman; I just used him for his money and whatever else I could get out of him. When he got his lawsuit money, he came upstairs to my apartment and asked me how much money I wanted. I told him I wanted a thousand dollars. He went into his pocket, pulled out his money, counted out a thousand dollars, and handed it to me without asking for anything in return.

I asked him why he did things for me and why he never told me no when I asked him for something or to do something for me. He said it was because I was a single mother and he wanted to help me. I knew it was more than that. I asked him, if I asked him to marry me, what he would say. He said he would say yes.

Even though he had feelings for me, he never tried to come on to me sexually. He always respected me and treated me like a lady.

I felt justified in asking him for things as long as he understood that we could only be friends. I didn't care about his feelings; all I cared about was what he could do for me.

The Spirit of God would convict me because not only was I wrong for using Him; God wanted me to trust Him to supply my every need. Every time God tried to prove Himself to me, I would run to the gentleman and ask him to give me what I wanted or needed.

I had to wait a few months before I could get licensed to drive, so my children and I had to catch a ride to church with the gentleman who lived downstairs. I hated catching a ride to church with them because not only did they have bad body odor, but the car was nasty. The car smelled so bad that I would almost get sick to my stomach, but I put up with it because I loved God and wanted to go to church. I appreciated him taking me to church, but I still wanted my license and my own car.

When it came time for me to get my license, the gentleman helped me study for my test. He would ask me the questions from the driver's manual to make sure I knew the answers. He would also explain to me the things I didn't understand about driving.

My kids were tired of riding in the gentleman's nasty, smelly car. They were happy when they found out I was going to get my license. I explained to them the benefits of my getting my license. I told them we wouldn't have to ride to church with the gentleman anymore and that we could go when we were ready. Knowing this made them very happy and excited. I watched the excitement in their eyes as I studied for my written driving test.

When it was time for me to take the written part of my driving test, the gentleman took me to the motor vehicle department to take the test. The first time I took the test, I failed. I was very disappointed about failing the test because I felt I had studied so hard. I didn't let failing the test discourage me from getting my license; I just studied even harder. When I went the second time to take the written part of my driving test, I passed and received my driving permit. I was so happy that I couldn't wait to tell my children and my mother.

Before I got saved, I would drive with no license, so I already knew how to drive. The gentleman would let me drive his car while he rode in the passenger's seat so I could practice. I loved to drive, so whenever the gentleman and I would go to church, to the store, or somewhere, I would drive. Since he drove to make a living, he said he was glad I could drive because he was tired of driving all the time.

While I waited to take my driver's test, I came across a 1985 Volkswagen Jetta that I purchased for $800. The gentleman who lived downstairs from me had my car painted, and he had a stereo system put in it for me.

When it came time for me to take my driving test, my cousin took me because his car was more appropriate than the gentleman's car. I was nervous about taking the driving test because, again, taking tests always makes me nervous. Although I was nervous, I had confidence that I would pass the test because I knew how to drive. I drove well in the beginning, but as I went on, I began making simple mistakes, like not coming to a complete stop at the stop sign and failing to yield. As I approached the motor vehicle building, the instructor told me I had made a lot of mistakes and that he should fail me, but he wasn't going to because he felt I could handle myself on the road. With joy, I thanked him; then I went into the motor vehicle building to get my license.

Several days later, I put insurance on my Jetta. I had it registered, and it was ready for the road. My kids and I were so happy. Now we didn't have to ride in a car that stank, and we could come and go as we pleased. Once again, I was thankful to God for allowing me to accomplish another task.

After I started driving my own car I didn't see the gentleman much, except for when I needed something from him or when I went downstairs to his apartment to see why he had stopped coming to church.

After getting my car it wasn't long before I got a job at the Marriott Reservation Center. I hated sitting at a desk and making reservations, but I needed a job, so I did it. Most of the people who worked at the reservation center were young, and they were not saved. When they got mad at the people who called to make a reservation, they would put them on hold and curse. The place was wicked, but I knew God had me there for a reason.

Most of the young people there respected me as a Christian. They would come to me for advice, and it wasn't long before I began taking them to church with me one by one. Most of them were not churchgoers. It was a blessing to have them attend church with me so they could hear the word and have a chance to give their lives to the Lord.

My car started breaking down on me. Fixing it was very costly, so I decided to sell it. I paid $800 for my car. Because I had put a lot of money into the car I decided to sell it for one thousand dollars. I wasn't sure if I could sell it for that amount, but I took the chance anyway. I put the "for sale" sign in the window. It wasn't long before I found out that a couple at my job was in need of a car so they decided to buy my car.

After selling my car I bought a 1998 Hyundai Sonata. After purchasing the car I found out the car dealer had ripped me off. They charged me too much for the car, my interest rate was too high, and my brakes started squeaking.

Every time I put my foot on the brakes to stop my car the brakes would squeak. It was embarrassing, so I kept taking my car back to the car dealer to be fixed, but they never fixed it. I got tired of running back and forth to the car dealer for the same problem, so I stopped taking my car to them. I had to put up with the squeaky brakes because I didn't have the money for another mechanic to fix them. I didn't want to ask the man who lived downstairs for the money because the Spirit of God convicted me again. I wanted to depend on God instead of man to supply my needs.

My Regenerated Life Is for God's Glory

I loved the Lord and I wanted to please him. As I continued to attend church on a regular basis I made up my mind that I was going to do all I could to live upright before him.

On Friday nights while testimony service was going on, I would always stand and give my testimony about how God saved me, delivered me from drugs and healed my body of the HIV virus. I would also give my testimony about how God was constantly revealing himself to me and moving in my life.

As I continued to focus on living right before God, it wasn't long before the enemy set another trap for me and I fell right into it. A gentleman who was the nephew of a member of our church, came from the south and began attending services at our church.

He made it known he was in need of a job. I wanted carpet put down where I lived and the landlord said he was going to have some put down. I figured since the gentleman needed a job I would ask my landlord if the gentleman could put the carpet down for a reasonable price. My landlord agreed to let the gentleman do the work.

Each time the gentleman came to my apartment, we talked. I told him about myself and he told me what he wanted me to know about himself. He claimed the Lord sent him to NJ to get his wife who he thought was my Pastor's sister. He also said maybe he was mistaken since he had met me. I knew my Pastor's sister was not his type and she wasn't looking for a husband anyway.

I, on the other hand, was tired of being by myself, and I did want a husband, so I focused on getting one. Wanting a husband made me very vulnerable to whoever came along. The gentleman didn't have a job; he lived with his aunt, and when he walked, he limped. My kids didn't like him, especially my daughter.

It wasn't long before he and I committed fornication. When we did it the first time I told him I loved God and I wasn't going to continue sinning with him. A couple of weeks later, he asked me would I marry him and I said yes.

I wanted to make sure this was the person God wanted me to be with, so I decided to pray about him becoming my husband. I got up early one morning and went into the living room; I knelt down on my knees and prayed about him and me getting married. As soon as I asked God if he was the one I was to marry, I heard a voice that said, "Yes, he is to be my husband, and I should do whatever he tells me to do." As soon as I heard the voice, I jumped up off my knees. I didn't pray anymore I just believed what the enemy said. Later on in the day I told him God said he was to be my husband. He believed me when I told him. He began spending most of his days and nights at my apartment. We decided it would be cheaper and more convenient for him and me, if he moved into my apartment while we planned to get married. We knew we were living in sin, but we justified it because we believed God said we were to be husband and wife.

He was on disability because he had back problems and couldn't work, but he did get odd jobs fixing people's houses and working on their cars. He would bring the money to me so I could pay some bills, and the rest I saved so we could purchase our wedding rings.

I was so into the man that I didn't care how my children felt. I was only concerned about getting married. My son was easygoing, so he didn't care one way or the other, but my daughter began acting out because she didn't like him. The man said my daughter acted like she did because she had a crush on him, which I thought was ridiculous, but I still didn't pay his comment any mind because the devil had me blinded, and I thought I was in love. When I asked my daughter did she have a crush on him she said, "No, That ugly man"!

Later on into our relationship the Lord began showing me things about him that I didn't like. One day I was on my way home from taking care of business and I noticed him sitting in his truck at the ice cream parlor up the street from my house. When I noticed him I decided to stop to talk to him. I went up to the drivers side of the truck and said hello to him. When he looked at me I could tell the devil had whispered all kinds of things to him which caused him to wonder where I was and if I had been cheating on him. He asked me where I had been. When I told him I could tell he didn't believe me, but I didn't care because I knew I was telling the truth. I could tell he was in a bad mood so I left him alone and went home. He didn't show up until later that night. I believe he stayed away to get back at me because he really believed I had been doing something I had no business doing.

Another thing he kept doing was bringing up the pastor's sister who he thought God sent him to NJ to marry. He did this to try to make me jealous. It worked because I started feeling insecure about our relationship and having resentment toward the pastor's sister who in reality had done nothing to me.

During Sunday morning service the Pastor Brown preached a sermon about fornication that really convicted me. I felt really bad so I decided to stop fornicating, but as soon as church was over my boyfriend rushed up to me to talk me out off my decision to stop sinning with him. I allowed the devil to come and immediately steal the word of God that came to convict me of my sins, and so I continued living in sin.

I thought I was happy, but I wasn't. I love God and I knew I wasn't living right. All I could think about was getting married so I didn't have to commit fornication anymore. I wanted to be able to testify with a clear conscious.

I always said that I would never testify about committing fornication because I knew if my pastor found out he would tell me not to sing in the choir, stop me from ushering and tell me not to testify. This was the punishment for members who committed fornication or adultery. What really made the person feel bad was him preaching about it on Sunday morning. Then everyone would know what the person did. I didn't want to go through this so I tried to hide the fact that I was committing fornication.

My boyfriend had a picture of a wedding band he drew. He said God had given him the design in a vision. It reminded me of a crown with different color stones in it. We had to have the band custom made so we went to Perth Amboy, NJ to have a jeweler there make it. The jeweler said it would cost about six hundred dollars for him to make it. He put a down payment on the wedding band. After the wedding band was finished we went back to the jewelry store to pay the remaining balance that was due on it. We decided I would pay for the engagement ring with my credit card and he would pay me back when he got the money. We left both rings at the store so they could be sized to fit our finger. The first receipt the jeweler gave me was in my boyfriends name, but the second receipt for the total amount paid for both rings was put under my name. I put both receipts in my purse as we left the store.

A day or two later I was sitting up in my bed when I heard the Lord tell me to call off the wedding. I knew it was the voice of God because there is something about the voice of the Lord. When he speaks you will know it is him. I jumped up and called my boyfriend on his cell phone and told him I needed to talk to him. When he came to my apartment I told him the Lord told me to call off the wedding and I couldn't marry him. He became very angry because he didn't want to call off the wedding. I on the other hand had made up my mind to obey God and call off the wedding and there was nothing he could say that could change my mind.

I told my ex-boyfriend I wanted him and his things out of my house. He told me that he wasn't going anywhere. I went in the room where his things were so I could get him to remove them from my apartment. He threw me on the bed and we began to tussle. I was trying to get him off of me so I pushed him in the face with the palm of my hands and in doing so I scratched him by mistake. He finally decided to get off of me and as I looked him in the eyes all I could see was evil. I began to plea the blood of Jesus against him. Each time I called on the name of Jesus he would take a step backwards. I then ran in my room and called the police.

When the police came I told them what happened and that I wanted him out of my house. He told the police he rented a room from me and took them in the room to show them his belongings. The police came out of the room and asked me were those his things in the room? I told them yes they were but he was not renting a room from me, he was lying. The police officer told me because his things were there that I couldn't just throw him out. The officers told me I would have to take him to court to have him removed from the premises. I insisted that he was lying, but they wouldn't listen to me.

The police officer noticed the scratch on my ex-boyfriends face where I had accidentally scratched him while trying to get him off of me. They asked me did I scratch him and I told them yes I did it by accident while trying to get him off of me. The officer explained to me that if I admitted putting the scratch on him they would have to lock me up for assault. The officer asked me again did I put the scratch on him and I told them that I was a Christian and I wasn't going to lie and that I put the scratch there by mistake trying to get him off of me. The officer told me I was under arrest for assault.

I asked the officer could I call my mother so she could come stay with my children because I didn't want to leave my ex-boyfriend in my apartment with my children. I called my mother and told her the police was arresting me for scratching my ex-boyfriend in the face by mistake. I also told her the police were not going to make him leave my apartment and I asked her would she come stay with my children until I came back home.

When my mother arrived at my apartment she began fussing with the cops for arresting me and not making my ex-boyfriend leave my apartment. She told the police officers that the apartment was in my name and that his name wasn't on the lease so he should have to leave. The cops told her to be quiet or else she would be getting arrested also.

There were two cops at my apartment. One was a little nicer than the other. The nicer police officer was the one who took me to the police station to be booked. On the way to the police station I explained to the officer my intentions and how I had made a big mistake getting involved with my ex-boyfriend. The police officer told me not to worry. He said he would tell the judge I co-operated with him and he would see if the judge would let me out without setting a bail.

When we arrived at the police station the officer told me to take my shoestrings out of my shoes and give them to him. He asked me did I have anything else in my possession. I told him no! He sat me in a chair next to his desk so he could write up my paper work. After all the paper work was done he put me in a jail cell while he went to speak to the judge on my behalf. I ended up staying in the cell for no more than a half an hour. Then the officer gave me a ride back home.

When I arrived home my mother and my ex-boyfriend were sitting on the steps. When my ex-boyfriend saw me get out of the police car, he started walking toward his truck.

When I got upstairs to my bedroom I realized my ex-boyfriend had went in my purse and took the receipts for the wedding rings. I checked my change bottle I had in my closet and he had taken most of my change I had saved up. I ran downstairs and told my mother what he had done. She said I should have told her I left my purse and change upstairs then she would have kept an eye on him.

I was concerned about the receipts for the rings because I had purchased one of the rings myself. I didn't know whether I should just let him keep the receipt so he could go get the rings and keep them for himself, or should I try to get back the ring I paid for with my credit card. My mother told me I should not let him get the ring I paid for. She told me I should go to the jewelry store and get my ring.

The following morning I drove to Perth Amboy to try and get the ring I paid for. When I arrived there my ex-boyfriend was there before me. He was sitting in his car waiting for the jewelry store to open. I parked behind him because I was going to wait right there with him. As I sat in my car I decided I would stop the police officer who was walking down the street and explain to him what was going on. I told the officer what happened and how my ex boyfriend was trying to take possession of both rings. I told the officer I didn't want the ring my ex-boyfriend paid for. All I wanted was my ring I paid for with my credit card.

My ex-boyfriend got out of his truck and showed the officer the receipt he had with his name on it. He also told the police he paid for both rings. I told the officer he was lying and he had another receipt with my name on it. The officer told us to wait until the jewelry store opened then he would get to the bottom of things. The officer said if I paid for one ring I would get the ring I paid for and my ex-boyfriend would get the ring he paid for.

When the jewelry store opened the police officer went in the store and asked the store's owner who's name the rings were under and if I paid for one of the rings with my credit card. The store owner confirmed what I had told the police. The police officer came out and told my ex-boyfriend that he should be glad I was being honest because by law I could have gotten both rings because both rings were in my name. The officer explained to us that I would get the ring I paid for and my ex-boyfriend would get the ring he paid for, but we would have to come back to pick them up when they were finished. The following week I went back to Perth Amboy and picked up my ring.

I didn't want my ex-boyfriend coming to my house bothering me, so I took out a restraining order against him. I wanted to be fair so I made sure I told the police officer who wrote up the restraining order and that my ex-boyfriend and I attended the same church. He said since it was a public place he could come to church as long as he didn't bother me.

When my ex-boyfriend was served with the restraining order, he went to the pastor and told him about our affair. Of course, he made himself look like the saint and made me out to be the bad person. My pastor phoned my house to talk to me. I told him my side of the story. My pastor asked me if I had committed fornication with him. I told him yes that I knew I was wrong and I had asked the Lord to forgive me.

My Pastor told me he was very disappointed with me and that he wanted me to sit out of the choir, not to usher and not to testify for a while until he could see the spirit of God moving upon me again. I don't know what he meant by that, but I agreed to follow his orders because I wanted to be obedient.

The following Friday I went to church and I sat quietly while testimony service was going on. I felt ashamed, embarrassed and I was burdened. I felt worse when I left church than I did when I got there.

When Sunday came I made a decision not to go to church because I knew the sermon was going to be about me committing fornication. Sunday night as I laid in my bed weeping, the Lord spoke to me and said and I quote "Not singing in the choir and not ushering is one thing but it was me who raised you up for a testimony for my glory". When God told me that I decided not to go back to that church.

My ex-boyfriend's aunt called me to find out why I didn't come to church that Sunday. I told her I would not be coming back and the reason why. I asked her what the message was about Sunday morning because I wanted to know if my instincts were right about the message being about me and what I had done. She told me he preached about fornication. She also told me I should have been there because I needed to hear the message. I was glad I didn't go to church because I would have felt worse than I already did.

The pastor heard that I would not be coming back to

church. The following Sunday when I didn't show up for church the pastor called me to find out for himself if I would be coming back or not. He said he needed to know if I would be coming back or not because he wanted to know whether to take my name of the roll. I told him to take my name off because I would not be coming back to his church.

I was very hurt because of the way the pastor dealt with me. He was so quick to punish and condemn me before finding out whether or not I was sorry and repented for what I had done. I also felt as though he sided more with my ex-boyfriend. I was a member at a church for five years. He never had to address the act of fornication with me before, even though I did need deliverance.

Before I sinned, the Spirit of God was telling me it was time for me to leave the church but because God told me when I first got saved that this was the church he wanted me to attend, I thought I was suppose to stay there. I didn't understand at the time I was only there for a season and it was time for me to move on and go to my next level.

I don't blame Pastor Brown for punishing me the way he did because he was only doing things the way he was taught. I also appreciate him for nurturing me and watching over me as a babe in Christ.

At the time I believed the apostolic church to be the only denomination who served God the right way. I didn't know of another apostolic church so I felt it would be better if I stayed home than go to another church.

After two weeks of not going to church, I received a phone call from a brother who was a member of the church I left. He told me, he and five other people had also left the church I left. He invited me to attend a church service that was going to be held in Old Bridge at one of the brother's houses who had also left the church. I asked him why they left the church and he told me our old pastor was a Trinitarian who believed in the Father, Son and Holy Ghost. I decided to take him up on his offer and go.

I was very uncomfortable in the service. I felt unworthy to praise God and to testify because of what I had done and the punishment I received at the other church, forbidding me to testify, to sing in the choir, or to usher. Most of the brother's and sister's had heard my testimony and they knew it was not like me to sit down and not say anything during testimony service so they encouraged me to stand and give my testimony. The devil was trying to steal my testimony and stop my praise, but with lots of prayer and encouragement I stood up and gave my testimony to the glory and honor of God. Service was very good. I didn't feel the same after service was over. I felt like a weight was lifted off of me.

After service, we had refreshments as we sat around and talked about what happened to me and why everyone else left the other church. We also talked about how powerful the Spirit of God had moved at a service held earlier during the week at the same brother's house.

One of the ladies said God had spoken to her and said seven people would be involved in starting this ministry, and my being there made me the seventh person. I wanted to be a part of a ministry, so I joined in and decided to help start the ministry. The gentleman at whose house we were would be the Pastor.

We continued to have service at the Pastor's house until I realized it would be a good idea to ask my landlord if we could have services in the basement of the house I lived in since it wasn't being occupied. I called my landlord and asked him could we use the basement to hold church services. I told him we would pay him rent and the electric bill. At first he said no because he didn't have insurance to cover anyone in case they got hurt. I was very disappointed with his answer, but I didn't give up on the idea. I decided to go to God in prayer about the matter. After prayer the Lord instructed me to ask him again. When I asked him again he agreed to let us use the basement at no charge. He didn't even charge us for use of the electricity.

We cleaned up the back yard and the basement, purchased chairs for the sanctuary, prayed over and decorated the basement to look and feel like a place of worship. We had a drum set, tambourines and a guitar for music.

Even though the basement was small we managed to hold all three Sunday school classes there. Each group spoke low enough not to disturb the next group. I loved going to Sunday school because we had dynamic teachers who knew the word, had revelation knowledge of the scriptures and was anointed to teach. Our pastor was anointed to teach the word. I gained a lot of knowledge at bible study that I had not learned during the five years at the other church.

The best part of the service was when the message went forth. The Word of God was so powerful and uplifting. I never experienced hearing the Word of God in that magnitude before. A few of the messages I'll never forget are: It's Only a Test; Where is the Glory and Chosen by God. Our spirit was being filled and we were very excited! We worshiped God from the depths of our hearts. We never began a service unless we set the atmosphere with worship. Services were powerful! God would show up and show out. The anointing was upon us so powerfully in some of the services. When it came time to leave we couldn't. Sometimes we dismissed the service while the Spirit of God was still moving upon us.

After one particular service I went to the closet to get my coat so I could go upstairs to my apartment. As I reached for the door knob to open the closet door, the Spirit of God took control of me. I began dancing in the Spirit all over again.

When I was a member at the other church my son along with most of the young people received the gift of the Holy Ghost. My daughter was very shy so she never tarried to be filled.

A brother at our church was good with working with people as they tarried for the Holy Ghost. I remember him and others praying and working with my daughter to be filled with the Holy Ghost. It seemed like she would never get it. I bowed my head and told God that he promised me my whole household would be saved. When I looked up my daughter was speaking in tongues as the Spirit gave her utterance. I was happy as I praised God for hearing and answering my prayer.

When my daughter and I went upstairs to our apartment, we were getting ready to go to bed. My daughter was so excited about receiving the gift of the Holy Ghost that she got a piece of paper and wrote down the date and day she got filled and before getting into bed she fell to her knees with excitement and said her prayers.

I've learned since then "to tarry" means to wait on God with expectancy and we don't have to beg God for anything. All we have to do is ask in faith and we shall receive.

During another service God used me to preach the Word. I didn't know I was going to speak. I stood up during testimony service to give my testimony and the Holy Ghost took over. Before I knew it the pastor's wife handed me the microphone and I preached the message that night. It was the first time I had ever spoken in front of a congregation. Whenever I stood in front of a large group of people to speak I would get nervous so I always tried to avoid doing it. This night God really used me. I stood up preaching under the anointing and didn't get nervous. I preached without realizing what I was doing. I just said what the Lord wanted me to say.

The pastor was the type of person who smiled when God

moved. I remember him smiling and saying God hadn't given him a message to preach because He had plans to use me to bring forth the message for that night. We continued to worship God in the basement and God continued to send people into our services. Most of the children were children I brought to church in my car. I went from house to house picking up children in my car. Eventually there were too many children to pick up so I had to pack them in my car like sardines, drop some off, then go back and pick more up. I realized I needed a bigger vehicle to transport the children. I wasn't working at the time so I knew I couldn't afford to trade my car in for a van. God was the only one who could meet this need for me so I turned to him for help.

I woke up one morning at 5:00 a.m. I felt a heaviness in my spirit to pray for a van to transport the children and others to church in. I knelt down by the side of my bed and prayed. I asked God to bless me with a van so I could bring people to church in. I thanked God for answering my prayer. Then I got up off my knees and went back to bed.

The following week I was taking my cousin and a lady from our church to look for a job. We were on Livingston Ave when the school crossing guard stepped out in the road, put up his stop sign for us to stop, so the children who were on their way to school could cross the street. I stopped and as I was waiting for the children to cross the street a man driving a Mark IV hit me in the rear on my passengers' side. He hit me so hard I jerked forward. A lady from my church who was in the front seat flew forward and my cousin, who was in the back seat, on the passenger's side, flew between the two front seats. After I realized what happened I got out of the car to see what damage was done to my car. The man hit me so hard his front left side bumper was wedged into my right rear end on the passengers' side. I didn't get mad because as soon as I saw the damages the

Lord spoke to me and said “your van is on the way”. I began leaping and praising God. Who ever was around must have thought I was crazy or something. When the police officer came I gave him my license, registration and insurance card. The cars had to be separated with a tow truck and towed away.

When the ambulance came my cousin and the other passenger were taken out of my car and placed in the back of the ambulance. I was hurt but I didn’t realize it, because I was so excited about my van. I called my aunt to tell her what happened. She told me to make sure I get into the ambulance so I could get checked out too. She said most of the time people don’t realize they’re hurt until the next day. I took her advice and went in the ambulance. When we arrived at the hospital after sitting around for a while my neck, back and finger started hurting. After being seen by the emergency room doctor I found out my finger was fractured. I was given a neck brace and pain medication. I was instructed to follow up with a back and neck doctor. I got the most injuries. My cousin’s back was injured and the other ladies’ wrist was hurt.

After the insurance company inspected the damages done to my car they totaled it out and paid the bank book value for my car. The book value was less than what I owed on my car, so I ended up owing an additional two thousand on the car.

I have an aunt who knows how to conduct business. We were on the phone talking about the accident and she suggested that I go back to the dealership where I purchased my vehicle to find out if I had insurance put on my car through the dealership (I forget the type of insurance it was). She said if I did the insurance was added onto the purchase price of the car and I should get a refund because the insurance was no longer needed. I did what she told me to do and to my surprise they had to give me back a thousand and some odd dollars. In addition to getting back my insurance money, God fixed it further. The insurance company who had paid off my car told me I could have the car after they had totaled it out and paid the book value of the car. I sold the car for fifteen hundred dollars. When God finished blessing me, I was able to pay what I owed on the car and still have money left over. If that wasn't good enough a friend of mine let me use his car to get around, at no cost, until I was able to purchase another vehicle. I was only without a car for about a month.

My daughter's father came to New Jersey from North Carolina to visit me, her and my son. While he was there I asked him to take me around to look for a van. We went around to several different car dealerships to no avail. He told me it was going to be hard for me to find a decent van for what I was willing to pay. Still determined I told him to keep his eye open for me and if he came across a used van to let me know. The following day he came by the house and told me he saw a van in Highland Park for fifteen hundred dollars.

The next day I went to look at the van. It was an ugly Astro van. I didn't like the vans because it was too square, but I figured it was better than nothing so I told the car dealer I would be back the next day with the money to purchase the van. I didn't feel comfortable about purchasing the van but I was still willing to buy it, but not without talking to God first. I asked God if it was his will for me to get the van to let it be there when I went back to purchase it, and if it wasn't meant for me to purchase it to let it be gone. I knew how much I was getting back from my income tax return so I asked my pastor if I could borrow fifteen hundred dollars from the church so I could purchase the van. I told him I would pay the church back as soon as I received my income tax check. I signed a paper stating the terms of the loan. Then he handed me a check written out with the church's name on it for fifteen hundred dollars.

The next day when I went to purchase the van it was gone so I knew that wasn't the van God wanted me to get. I continued looking for a van in the price range of a thousand to fifteen hundred dollars.

I didn't think the dealership would approve me for a newer van because I didn't have a job. With this in mind I only looked for vans in the price range of a thousand to fifteen hundred dollars. Finding a decent van in this price range was very difficult because all the decent vans were $3,000 and up. I knew what God told me when I had the car accident concerning the van so I knew I was going to get one. However finding a van in the price range I wanted was frustrating. I decided to stop looking for it that day and try again the next day.

The next day I asked a brother from my church if he would go around with me to try and find a van. We decided to go to a Saturn dealer. We saw a 1998 green Nissan Quest van that was in good shape. The brother from my church suggested to me that I should get the van. Although I was reluctant to purchase a van that I had to make a monthly payment on, I took his advice and decided to try to get the van. I didn't have a job but I had a check with the church's name on it. I decided to tell the salesman that I worked for the church and use the check for proof of income. Even though I did work at the church I was still telling a lie because I didn't get paid for working at the church. My work at the church was voluntary as service rendered unto God. I was approved for the van but I couldn't take the van home. It was late and I didn't have insurance on the van so I had to come back the next day and pick the van up.

On my way home, the spirit of God began reminding me of the lie I told about working for the church. I felt so bad that I called another brother from the church and told him what I had done. He called the pastor and told him what I had done, then called me back and told me the pastor said I shouldn't have lied about working for the church. When I got home, I went in my bedroom, got on my knees, and asked God to forgive me for telling a lie. Then I called the salesman at the car dealership and told him I had lied about having a job and that I wouldn't be able to purchase the van. The salesman thanked me for my honesty and said it wasn't a problem; I could still pick the van up in the morning. The next day, when I went to pick the van up it was cleaned and ready for me to drive home.

Having a van allowed me to bring more children to church without having to make lots of trips back and forth to pick them up and take them home again. God also blessed me with a job working part-time at the Pepsi-Cola Company in Piscataway. I was able to meet my monthly car payments. When my income tax check came I paid the church back the fifteen hundred dollars that I borrowed.

Because I told the truth about not having a job or working for the church, I was able to give my testimony about how God had blessed me with my van and a job to pay for it. I realized that if I hadn't told the truth about not working for the church, the devil would have robbed me of my testimony. I learned that God doesn't need my help when He wants to bless me and that He is able to bless me beyond measure. All I have to do is stand on God's word no matter what the situation looks like.

My son became unhappy about something the pastor said to him and decided to bring it to my attention. My son said the pastor told him that if he didn't let his two sons play his drums, he was going to make him take his drum set back upstairs to our apartment. I told my son that he should take turns with the pastor's sons, and it would be fair if each of them played two songs and then switch with the next person. My son said he did take turns, but they were trying to take over the drums. I told my son that he should not let them take over but he should share. I felt bad about the threat the pastor had made to my son so I decided to talk to him about it. I explained to the Pastor that I didn't think it was right to threaten my son. I felt he should have dealt with the situation a different way rather than threatening my son. My son is not a selfish person and he didn't mind sharing, but he felt the pastor's sons were trying to take over his drum set. I then expressed my opinion by suggesting that he should set up a fair time for each of them to play by letting each of them play for two songs and then switch. The pastor agreed and the three boys began taking turns playing.

Lord, I Want A Nice Apartment With A Walk-in Closet!

I had an apartment on the second and third floor of a two family house. I had two bedrooms, a kitchen, a full bathroom and a living room on the second floor. On the third floor I had two bedrooms, a sitting room and another full bathroom. The apartment had plenty of room space, but I still wasn't happy with it because the closets and bathrooms were too small and the outside of the house looked very bad. The siding on the house was falling off and the yard was too small for the children to play in. The outside of the house looked so bad that people thought the inside of the house was a mess too. I knew they thought this way because of the reaction on their face when they walked into my apartment and saw that it was clean. One person even told me because of the way the outside of the house looked they thought my apartment was messy also.

I asked the landlord several times when was he going to fix the outside of the house. He always said soon, but never got around to doing it. I was tired of the small closet space in the house and the way the outside of the house looked, so I prayed.

I asked God for a nicer apartment with a large master bedroom, with my own private bathroom and more closet space. Within a couple of months I felt very strongly in my spirit that it was time for me to move. I called my section eight worker and told her I wanted to move. She told me I had to give my landlord a two months notice prior to moving out. She instructed me to find an apartment and then come to her office and pick up a rental voucher so the new apartment owner could fill it out.

I called my landlord and told him I would be moving out. He asked me why? I told him it was because of how the outside of the house looked and I needed more closet space. He stated he didn't want me to move out. He said he was going to get around to fixing the outside of the house very soon. I sympathized with him and agreed to continue living in the apartment.

One reason I agreed to stay in the apartment was because when I was on drugs and at the lowest point in my life he did not turn me away. He rented me the apartment even though he knew I was on drugs. Hearing him say he didn't want me to move, kind of made me feel like I was deserting him.

I continued to live in the apartment for a couple months. The Spirit of God kept telling me to move. I tried to ignore the Spirit of God, but when God wants you to do something He will keep at you until you do it. God wanted me to have better and it was time for me to move on.

Before calling my landlord to give him my two months notice I went to a brand new apartment complex that had just been built. The apartment was very nice. It had a large master bedroom with its own bathroom in it, with a large walk-in closet, the bedrooms were roomy with plenty of closet space. The kitchen had a dishwasher, nice stove and refrigerator and plenty of cabinet space to store my food. There was a small dining room, a nice size living room with a balcony with sliding doors.

The apartment complex had middle class tenants. Most of the people who lived there had money. One month's rent for a three bedroom apartment cost $1400. In order for me to rent the apartment with my section eight voucher I would have to come up with a month and a half security deposit and have a job.

When I saw the apartment I knew it was the one for me and I was determined to get it. I called my section eight worker and told her where I wanted to move. She made an appointment to meet with me. After meeting with her she informed me that she would have to take a close look at my income before determining if I could get the apartment. After taking a close look at my income she said I would be cutting it close, but she would see what she could do.

I believed God for my new apartment and called my landlord by faith, giving him my two months' notice. He tried to talk me out of moving, but I insisted it was time for me to move on. He became angry because he didn't want to have to go through painting the house and finding another tenant so soon. To try and repay him for helping me at the lowest point in my life, I promised him I would find another decent, trustworthy tenant to move into the apartment. My brother and his wife wanted to move from where they were living so they agreed to move into the apartment after I moved out.

My Section Eight worker approved the apartment. After I cleaned it, my brother helped me move my heavy furniture with a U-Haul truck, but I had to move the rest of my belongings by myself. I had to make three trips with my van. I had to carry my things down two flights of steps at the old house and up one flight of steps into my new apartment. When I got to the last load, I was so tired that I had to pay a young man, who was an alcoholic, twenty dollars to help me move. I didn't want him to help me because I didn't want to contribute to his drinking, but I had no choice. He was the only person willing to help me, and I was so tired.

Before I gave him the money, I told him, This is God's money and if I were you I wouldn't buy alcohol with it because you never know what might happen. He was very respectful and agreed not to buy alcohol with the money. The next day when I saw the young man I noticed he had a busted lip and a cracked tooth. "You got drunk anyway didn't you?" I asked He said yes. I didn't mean to laugh at him but I did anyway. He looked funny and I warned him not to use the money to buy alcohol.

One day, I was going into my walk-in closet to get something out, and as I entered, the Lord began to minister to me about how I had prayed to Him, asking Him for an apartment with a walk-in closet and how He had answered my prayer. The Spirit of praise took over, and I began to praise God all through my apartment for answering my prayers, delivering me from drugs, and setting me free from sin.

We continued to have our church services in the basement of the old house I moved from. I left my son's drum set in the basement because I didn't have anywhere to put them in my new apartment and the church still had need of them. The church was slowly growing. There were about six to seven other adults who had joined the ministry. There were now fourteen adults. I spent most of my time with my church family so I felt very close to them. As a matter of fact spiritually they were my family.

Three of the members started hanging out alot with the pastor and his family. The pastor and his family would invite them to eat at their house on some Sundays and on other Sundays the pastor and his family would go to the other couples house to eat. The sister who lived with me, and I were never invited to eat dinner with them so she and I would make dinner for us. Sometimes my children and I, the lady who lived with me and the gentleman who played the guitar for our church would go out to the Chinese Restaurant and eat dinner together. She and I would talk about how we felt about not ever being invited to the pastor's house for dinner. Several times I even cooked dinner and invited the pastor and his family over for dinner. Even though we didn't like being left out we didn't let that stop us from doing our part in the ministry.

When Thanksgiving came, everyone from our congregation except me and another member were invited to the pastor's house for Thanksgiving dinner. I was very hurt because I felt left out. I felt they should have invited everyone. I ended up spending Thanksgiving dinner home alone because no one in my family invited me to dinner either.

I don't like it when church members have cliques because it make the others who are not in the cliques feel left out and unloved. We didn't have but a few members so when some of them started hanging together it was very noticeable.

When Sunday morning came I didn't go to church. I was sick from being so angry and harboring unforgiveness in my heart. After morning service all the members who normally went to the pastor's house for dinner came to my house to check on me. I was always one who said exactly how I felt. I held resentment toward my church family for having cliques for a long time and I didn't even know it. When they came to my house I started yelling and telling them how I felt about having cliques and not inviting me to eat thanksgiving dinner with them. The pastor said if he had known I felt the way I did he would have invited me. He also said he figured I would be eating thanksgiving dinner with my family and that's why he didn't invite me. I didn't want to hear what he had to say because I felt he knew I spent most of my time with them working in the ministry and I didn't feel close to my biological family anyway. The pastor's wife told her husband they should leave and one of the other members commented that it was the pastor's and his wife's business who they invited to their house for dinner anyway. I made up my mind not to go back to the church. I went to the church and took my tambourine and my son's drum set from the basement.

I wouldn't go to a church if it wasn't an apostolic church because I was taught if a church wasn't apostolic they believed in three God's and the people weren't saved. I couldn't find another apostolic church where I lived. I was out of church for several Sundays.

I remembered an apostolic preacher coming to the first church I attended for five years, so I decided to give his church a try. The church was located in Roselle, NJ. The first time I went to the church the Pastor was preaching a sermon and because the word was in me, I felt the presence of God. I figured if I felt the power of God there it was a good sign so I joined the church. After joining the church I began to see a lot of things in the church that weren't right. As I continued to attend the church I became weaker and weaker in the spirit. The pastor would do things to try and break a person's spirit opposed to feeding their spirit. I have to let the truth be told. It was as if the pastor didn't want the members to grow because if they did they would have seen he was walking in the flesh.

God began to deal with me on how I had left the other two churches. I mentioned it to the pastor. I told him I had to go back and apologize. The pastor asked me did I do anything wrong. I told him not that I knew of but the way I left wasn't right. He said if I didn't do anything wrong then I had no need to apologize. I knew God was telling me to go back and apologize so that's what I did.

I went to a Friday night service at the first church I attended and stood up during testimony service and apologized for the way I left. Then I told everybody I loved them. It was a big relieve off of me and God was teaching me to forgive. Now I was free to visit the church if I choose to and from time to time I would call the pastor to see how him and his family were doing. I didn't go to the other church, but I did call the pastor and his wife and apologize to them over the phone for getting upset about not being invited to their thanksgiving dinner.

While I attended the church in Roselle I rode on a plane for the first time in my life. I went to a conference in Palm Beach, Florida and the second time I took a plane to South Carolina to attend a youth conference with the pastor and some of the children from our church.

At the conference in Palm Beach, Florida there were white apostolic church people who were prejudiced. I couldn't believe what I was seeing! People who called themselves saved, sanctified and filled with the Holy Ghost walked past us African American Christians and would not speak. The first thought that came to mind was did they really think they were going to make it into heaven with hate in their hearts.

The pastor made an announcement in church that the church was in need of a secretary. The former secretary had gotten upset with the pastor and quit. I was in need of some extra money. Since I had some secretarial training and I was in need of some extra money, I decided to put in for the job.

After meeting with the pastor and answering a few questions he gave me the job. I had to travel from Somerset to Roselle for about one month which took about thirty to forty minutes each way to work about four to five hours a day. After getting to work there really wasn't much to do because things were not organized. The computer didn't have the proper software to store the church information. For instance, I could not keep a record of who paid tithes for the year and how much was paid. There was no financial record of anything. People wanted copies of how much in tithes they had paid, but I couldn't give it to them because no one had kept record.

Every time someone asked the pastor for a record of how much in tithes they had given for the year, he would tell them he was getting a program for the computer so he could give it to them. The pastor did several things that weren't right. Not getting my tithes financial report didn't bother me because I never filed income tax.

A man called to the church and said the pastor owed him money for some books he had gotten from him on credit. The man said he had a son who was ill and he had to take care of him so he said he was going out of business. He wanted to collect the money that was owed him for his son's medical bills. My pastor was in New York so I called him on his cell phone and told him what the man said. My pastor told me to tell the man he would pay him when he returned home. When the pastor came home from his trip to New York I reminded him about owing the gentleman. The pastor told me not to worry about the man. He wasn't important and never paid the man. The pastor told the man a lie and I felt bad about it.

Working for the pastor was very stressful and aggravating. It was as if he was trying to push my last buttons. He would tell me to do lots of tasks at one time and he didn't give me time to finish them and most of the task weren't important.

Marriage, Lies And Deception

When I started dating my ex-husband, my heart was set on getting a husband and not totally on God and his will for my life. Because of that, I ended up falling and having sex with him. He was my boyfriend at the time. After having sex with him I felt bad and cried to the Lord and asked him to forgive me like I always did when I committed fornication. It was like a vicious cycle that kept repeating itself. I would commit fornication, feel bad about it, weep before God and ask him to forgive me. In my heart I wanted to live right before God, but I kept committing fornication. I never planned to do it. When the Lord would warn me not to go into an unsafe environment, I would disobey him and give in to my fleshly desires and go anyway.

Rumors started going around the church that someone had seen my van parked at my boyfriend's house late at night, So I told my boyfriend I wasn't going to sin with him any more. The more time we spent together the more we committed fornication. It was like we couldn't stay away from each other, so we decided it would be best if we got married.

Without praying we made plans to get married. My boyfriend told me to call the pastor and tell him we wanted to get married and to ask him would he counsel us.

When I called the Pastor and told him we wanted to get married and asked him if he would counsel us, he told me he wasn't going to counsel or marry us. He told me, he couldn't see us getting married and that my boyfriend had issues. I asked him what kind of issues did he have and he said he wasn't going to go into them with me. I suggested we all sit down and discuss the issues he was talking about, but he said if he sat down and talked to us it would be as if he was counseling us so he wasn't going to do it. He made another comment saying "If your boyfriend marry you he is a fool." Those words hurt me so bad that I hung the phone up and cried like a baby. I called the Pastor's wife on her job and explained to her what her husband said to me. She asked me was I sure that's what he said. I said yes. She said she would talk to him about his decision and about the comment he made to me.

I talked to my pastor's wife before talking to my pastor about our plans to get married. She warned me and another lady that her husband had a problem when it came to marrying couples in the church. However, we didn't think he would go so far as to making comments to make us feel bad. If the pastor felt we shouldn't get married I feel he should have sat us down and explained why, instead of handling it the way he did.

When we went to church for bible study the pastor stood before the congregation and talked about the conversation we had over the phone. He explained that he wasn't going to counsel or marry us or anyone that he felt weren't meant to be together. I couldn't believe what I was hearing because it wasn't anybody's business but ours. My spirit was crushed by the things he said and because of that I lost my trust in him.

All of the pastors I've sat under would get on the pulpit

and openly rebuke a person and make them feel bad. I feel what is discussed with a member and the pastor should stay between them unless the member was disobedient after speaking with the pastor and he or she is causing problems in the church. Because of the Pastor's actions, my fiancé and I decided to leave the church.

Afterward, the pastor would call me and talk bad about my fiancé' to me then he would call my fiancé while he was at work and talk bad about me to him. Not only was he trying to turn us against each other, but he was also trying to get my fiancé to come back to his church.

My fiancé and I went back to the church I attended prior to the church we just left. We explained to the pastor the reason we left the other church and how the pastor refused to counsel then marry us, and how he refused to even meet with us to explain why he felt we shouldn't get married. I also explained to the pastor that we had fallen several times and committed fornication and we felt it was best if we got married. This pastor agreed to counsel and then marry us.

While my fiancé and I waited to get married we continued to get to know one another, so I thought! While driving from his apartment to my apartment he told me one of his teachers did not want to pass him or give him his diploma when graduation time came. He said he told his brother what happened so his brother went up to the school and threatened to beat up the teacher if he didn't give his brother his diploma. He said that's how he received his diploma. At the time I didn't question him about why the teacher did not want to give him his diploma, but I knew there was a good reason.

He also told me that he had not yet gotten his drivers license. I asked him why. He said it was because he had failed the written part of the test and he never went back to retake it. His answer puzzled me and it did not set right in my spirit because I felt very few people didn't stop trying to get their license after the first time, if they really want their license. I kept going over it in my mind and asking him why he never went back to retake the test, but he would just sit there and not answer me. I told him after we were married he had to get his license right away because I didn't want to have to drive him around all the time. I wanted him to drive me around sometimes.

When we started our counseling the pastor had us write down what kind of wife and husband we were going to be to each other. The pastor collected the papers and went over them and at the end of the session he gave me my fiancé's paper and he gave my fiancé my paper. When I got home I looked over my fiancé's paper. When I tried to read it I found multiple spelling mistakes and broken sentences. I thought my fiancé' just had a spelling problem because some people are not good at spelling. I thought he could read because every time I saw him he had his bible opened as if he was reading it and he did the same thing with the newspaper so I didn't think twice about it.

My fiancé and I had to decide where we were going to live after we were married. We figured it would be better if we lived in my apartment in Somerset since my children were smaller and still in school. My fiancé has two children, a daughter who was seventeen at the time and an older son who lived away from home. When my fiancé asked his daughter did she want to come live with us after we were married she said she would rather stay with my fiancé's sister because she didn't want to live with me and my children. My fiancé agreed to let her live with his sister and pay for her room and board. His daughter had dropped out of school and was practically doing what she wanted to do anyway so I figured it was better that way.

I was concerned about the large amount of money he had to pay to his sister for his daughter because we had plans to buy a house after we were married. We needed to save all the money we could. Besides, I felt that if my fiancé's daughter was living like she was grown and had dropped out of school, she needed to get a job to take care of herself. When I explained how I felt about the situation, my fiancé said she was his daughter and he had to take care of her. He also told me not to worry about the money because he was a janitor at one of the schools in Linden, NJ and he received an incentive check for working during the summer months and we could save that money to purchase a home.

After our counseling sessions were over, we began making plans for the wedding. I planned to have four bridesmaids' and four male ushers, a flower girl, a ring bearer, a maid of honor and a best man. My fiancé's daughter was supposed to be one of the bridesmaids. When it came time for her to get fitted for her dress, she would never show up. Not only did I have problems with her, I had problems getting the other bridesmaids to show up for their dress fitting also. It became very frustrating, so I decided not to have any bridesmaids or ushers in my wedding

The church paid for the rental of a wedding site because we didn't have our own church building. My husband and I rented the firehouse for our reception. The church members provided the food and decorated the reception hall. My sister-in-law made the favors, and my aunt decorated the bride and groom's table. A lady who attended the church we left agreed to pick me up in her husband's off-white Jaguar.

We planned to invite only fifty people because the space at the firehouse was very small. We wanted to be fair toward one another, so we each were to invite twenty-five guests apiece. We ended up inviting more people than we planned because I had a big family. I didn't want to leave out any of my family who played a part in my life. My fiancé's family was small, but there were a lot of people he wanted to invite from the church he had attended. This included the pastor who refused to marry us and his wife. I didn't want them to attend my wedding because we didn't have their blessings. Out of respect for my fiancé, I invited them to stay away.

Our wedding ceremony turned out all right except for a few things. Most of my husband's family were late. They wore jeans, sneakers, and head rags. My husband never once looked at me as I walked down the aisle to him. He said the reason he didn't look at me was that his best man told him he shouldn't look at me while I walked down the aisle, so he didn't.

The pastor, whom I didn't want to invite, sat in the pews with his head down, pretending to read the ceremony program during the entire wedding. When my husband and I walked out of the church, he handed my husband a card with no money in it. I knew he was trying to be funny, but I didn't care because it showed how immature he was.

At the reception, my new husband's family sat with their backs toward the bride and groom table. None of them said anything to me, although my husband's brother did get up and give a small speech directed personally to his brother and then handed him a card with money in it.

When I stood to thank everyone for coming, my husband's daughter walked past me with a mad face and went to the bathroom. As I was talking, and when it was time for my husband and me to go around to each table to greet the guests, all of my husband's family left including my husband. My husband asked me if he could walk his daughter outside. I told him yes thinking he would be right back, but to my surprise he stayed outside for almost an hour talking to his family and left me to greet our guests by myself.

Out of all the things that happened during my wedding and the reception, the thing that hurt me the most was the fact that my husband never looked at me as I walked down the aisle to him. Then he left me to greet the guests alone. I wasn't bothered by what the other people did, but what my husband did bothered me. I felt he should have had enough sense to know that it was my day and that he should have stayed by my side.

I felt he cared more about how his daughter felt than about me. He didn't have enough sense to realize that his daughter was only trying to make him feel bad for marrying me, that she was trying to ruin my wedding day by acting immaturely.

A few weeks after my husband and I were married, I received a threatening phone call from one of my husband's sisters, threatening to call my Section 8 worker and tell her I was married and that my husband was living with me. Little did she know I had already told my case worker I was married and that my husband was living with me in my apartment. When her plan didn't work, my husband's family came up with another plan to try to split us up.

My husband's daughter called him at work and told him that when she was thirteen and living with him, she had been raped by her mother's brother. My husband's daughter knew her father loved her, so she wanted to manipulate him by telling him something that would make him believe he needed to be with her.

After my husband's daughter told him she had been raped, he became very upset. I never believed it to be true. On the other hand, I always felt in my spirit she only told him this to try to manipulate him, but I gave her the benefit of the doubt. I felt sorry for her because, if in fact it did happen to her, it was a terrible thing. I also felt sorry for my husband because, if it did happen, it happened while she was in his care. I know this made him feel like he didn't do his job as a father and protect her.

My husband and I were lying in bed one night discussing his daughter and what she said happened to her. I felt sorry for my husband, and I tried to comfort him by putting my hands around him to caress him, but he pushed me away. Then he got out of bed and told me he wasn't going to make love to me because of what had happened to his daughter.

I wasn't trying to make love to him. Even if I was, I felt he shouldn't have taken out on me what happened to his daughter. I got mad at him and threw a bottle of pills at him as he walked into the bathroom. I was trying to hit him in the head with it, but I missed. My husband and I argued for a while, and he ended up sleeping on the couch.

A week later, I went to a wedding at our church, and when I came home, my husband had taken all his belongings and left. He went to stay with his sister and his daughter in Elizabeth, NJ. Three days later, he phoned to tell me where he was. He told me he felt he should be with his daughter because of what had happened to her. He also told me we needed to date for a while before we lived together and that he had gone back to the church in Roselle. I told him I was his wife and that he needed to be with me and we needed to work through our problems together. I also told him I wasn't going to live like we were boyfriend and girlfriend because we were married. I told him not to call me unless he wanted to come back home and be a husband to me, like he vowed to do. He didn't take me seriously, and he would try to call me anyway. I would just hang up on him because I didn't want to talk to him. After my husband called me several times, I decided to talk to him. We made plans to meet at his job so we could sit down and talk and try to work out our disagreements.

One of my concerns was about his bonus check he said he would receive from his job during the summer. I hadn't seen a dime of it, so I asked him about it. My husband's response was that his job never gave it to him. Even though I thought he was telling me another lie, I let it go because I couldn't prove it. After a long talk with him, we still couldn't come to any mutual understanding. It was clear to me that my husband was set on putting his daughter and other family members before me. He should have known I wasn't going for that.

I agreed to drop my husband off at the bus stop so he could take the bus to his sister's house. On the way there, I used my cell phone to call a minister from my church so he could talk to my husband about his decision not to return home. With a lot of persuasion from the minister, my husband decided to come back home, and we made arrangements for me to pick up his things the following week from one of his family members' houses.

After my husband and I got back together, our relationship seemed like it was getting better. We began communicating more, and he tried to give me the love and affection I needed. I tried to respect him as the head of the household, but it was hard because he lacked leadership skills. My husband would always say he was the head because he was the man, but he didn't have a clue what duties came along with being the head of the household.

My husband never helped me make decisions concerning the household. I was tired of doing his job and mine. I felt like I had another child in the house instead of a husband, so I started feeling frustrated and stressed out again. I would express the way I felt by arguing and fussing at him. My husband would just walk away from me and mumble things under his breath. Sometimes my daughter would hear what he mumbled and tell me what he said. I would get even more upset with him and argue with him even more. I never stayed angry at my husband for long because God would deal with me and I would have to apologize to him.

God told me to have prayer and Bible study with my family. He told me to let each one of us take turns leading Bible study. We each were to pray, read a scripture, and expound on it. When it was my husband's turn, the children and I realized he couldn't read past a fourth-grade level. My son was so shocked that he sat there with his mouth open. Not long after, my son blurted out, "He can't read!" I shoved my son on the arm and told him to be quiet. Since we were already married when I found out my husband couldn't read, I decided to help him learn to read. I suggested that he and I read the Bible every night before going to sleep. I would let him read. When he didn't know a word, I would tell him what the word was. Every time I tried to tell him what the word was, he would cut me off by blurting out the word as if he knew how to pronounce it. My husband was full of pride, so I stopped reading with him.

Shake the dust off my feet!

My husband and I did not pray about going back to Word of Life Apostolic Church. We went there because we wanted to get married, and the pastor agreed to marry us. When we started going to the church, they were having service at the hotel on Sundays, and during the week, they had Bible study and prayer meetings in the garage of a lady's house. I have a friend who turned his living room and dining room into a place of worship so he could have church. He would let other churches come in at alternate times and have services. We were having our services in the hotel, and the cost was rather expensive. I figured it would be cheaper for us if I asked my friend if we could have our church services at his house; that way, we could save money to get our own church building someday.

When I asked my friend how much he would charge us to have services at his house, he said all he wanted us to do was help with the electric bill. We had Bible study one day a week, Sunday morning service, and Sunday evening services in his home. On the days we couldn't have services at my friend's house, we would have prayer and Bible study in the ladies' garage.

I was always one who loved church, and I loved to go to church for no other reason but to worship and praise God. Most of the time I went to church, I would close my eyes and worship God because I wanted to tune people out and focus on Him. However, even though I tried to tune them out, I still noticed a lot of things that weren't right.

Not only did I notice things in the church that weren't right, but I also had to deal with the fact that my husband was not comfortable at the church. He only went to make me happy. We continued to press our way to church, but the more we went, the more God would show me things in the church that weren't right. I was hesitant to leave because I was tired of going from one church to another.

Here we were living in America, surrounded by drug addicts, prostitutes, alcoholics, and people who just needed to be saved. I couldn't understand why the majority of our congregation was from Jamaica. I felt we should be able to witness and win the lost no matter where they were from. There was a lot of favoritism going on at the church. Jamaicans ran the church. Things had to be their way or no way.

Not only that, the pastor made comments like "these drug addicts and prostitutes" instead of saying "the unsaved" or just preaching the word of God and letting the Spirit of God draw them. They knew what they were; he didn't have to remind them. Words can be used to push people away, or words can be used to draw them near because death and life are in the power of the tongue, and they that love it shall eat the fruit thereof. (Proverbs 18:21) "The fruit of the righteous is a tree of life; and he that winneth souls is wise" (Proverbs 11:30). A Christian has to use wisdom if they want to win the lost. You can't say anything you want to say and in any way you want to say it.

Because of my background as a drug user and a prostitute, I knew the choice of words the pastor used was not wise. Hearing him talk like that grieved my spirit because God anointed me to win souls for Christ therefore I had a burden in my heart to see people saved and I knew he could not win souls for Christ saying things the way he did.

After talking with several people who lived in the house, I found out the comments he made only made them feel like they were not good enough to attend the same church as we were. I wanted to talk to the pastor about it, but I knew from past experiences with him that he thought he was right and others were wrong.

I often wondered if they really knew why God saved and delivered me from drugs, alcohol, and prostitution. I knew God did it for His glory, but I also knew He delivered me so I could identify with their situation, be a witness to them, and win them for Christ.

Even though my spirit was grieved and I found myself feeling as if we would not win the unsaved for Christ, I was determined to stay and worship at the church. I loved my brothers and sisters in Christ, and I was tired of running from one church to another, so I decided to try to eat the meat and spit out the bones. God was telling me He wanted me to leave that church and move on, but I ignored Him, so He allowed something to happen that would surely move me into my next spiritual level.

One day, as my children and I were driving home from church, my son asked, "Why did the pastor make me let his two sons play my drums at the other church, but when I want to play the drums now, he tells his son to play as long as he wants to, and then when he is tired, he can let me play?" I asked my son if he told the pastor how he felt. He said no because he was scared. I told my son I would address his concerns with the pastor because I wasn't going to let my son be treated unjustly. I also didn't think what he said was fair, nor was it setting a good example for the children. I always teach my children to share and to treat others the way they want to be treated. Adults have to be careful not to discourage children from using their talents. God gave my son the gift of playing the drums as a child, and I did not want him to become discouraged.

I spoke with a minister from the church about the situation; then he took it upon himself and spoke with the pastor about it. The Spirit of God informed me that the pastor was going to be defensive about the matter, and I knew when I went to church I was going to hear something relating to it coming from the pulpit. I didn't think it would come from the person to whom I had confided.

I told an evangelist who rode to the church with me about the situation because she was like a mentor to me. I was also the one who introduced her to the ministry because she too had left our prior church and was looking for a church home. She was asked to speak that night and to my surprise she talked about the very thing I had discussed with her in a round about way. I knew what she was talking about and who she was talking to. I felt hurt and betrayed because I love the evangelist and trusted her to minister to me the right way, but she didn't.

One may ask how I know it wasn't God speaking through her. One thing I've learned in my walk with God is to try the spirit by the spirit. I can discern when the Spirit of God convicts me, as opposed to a person speaking from their own flesh, and this was one of those times.

After she was through speaking, she came and sat back next to me. I didn't say anything to her about what she did. I made up my heart and mind that I wasn't going to hold it against her. I just continued to smile and praise the Lord.

We had prayer that night, and as I was on my knees praying, the Holy Ghost lifted up a standard within me and began to rebuke all the negative spirits that were trying to intimidate me from addressing the issue about the drums with the pastor. When I was finished praying, I could tell from the look on some of the saints' faces that they were shocked at my reaction in prayer.

After service had let out and I was through greeting some of the saints, I asked the pastor if I could speak with him alone. He and I went into a room leading out of the church, and I told him my son asked me why he told his son to play the drums until he was tired and then, if he wanted to, he could let my son play. He told me it was because his son was the drummer. I then reminded him about how he dealt with the situation when his sons wanted to play my son's drums while my son was the drummer. He told me because that was then and this is now.

I began to explain to him how I didn't feel it was right the way he dealt with the children and that he should treat them equally. The pastor got offended, raised his voice, and told me, "I'm the pastor!" Immediately, I became upset and began to defend myself. I asked him, because he was the pastor, did he think it was right for him to treat people any kind of way? He began yelling at me, so I yelled at him. I know for a fact he knew if he yelled at me that I was going to yell at him back and he did it because he wanted it to seem as though I was being disrespectful to him as the pastor.

He and I passed words back and forth as I headed toward the door. I could feel and hear the Spirit of God as I walked out, shaking the dust off my feet and telling me not to go back to the church.

As I came closer to the door the pastor's wife came to where we were along with the other members of the church. She told her husband to be quiet and as she asked me in a concerned voice what the problem was, I tried to explain to her but with other people trying to interfere it was hard. Another lady came and blocked the door unintentionally trying to find out what was wrong. I didn't think what she thought mattered to me since she was very close to the pastor anyway. I felt she would have seen things his way anyway even if he was wrong. The pastor's wife instructed her to leave me alone and I left.

As I sat waiting for the evangelist who rode with me to church to come out of the church, the owner of the house, who had overheard the argument but didn't know exactly what happened, told me I knew better than to argue with the pastor. I knew he was right, but I also felt I was provoked, and I had not acquired self-control yet. I also knew he was a wise man, and I could talk to him when we were alone and when I was a little calmer.

I never went back to church there, although I did go back to my friend's house to sit and talk with him about what happened. I can say he is a very wise man who knows how to talk to me and get me to see my wrongs, and he also understands why people do things that are not right and can be provoked to anger. I thank God for him because he has taught me a lot before and after I gave my life to the Lord.

Looking back on the whole situation, I realize God was trying to take me into another season and level in my life, and it wasn't going to happen at the church I was in. Because I was determined to stay, God allowed something to happen so I would leave the church and move on.

You Can't Hide from God

I received a lump sum of money from my disability claim. I figured that since my husband and I had a little money, it would be good for us to take a vacation together, since we didn't have a honeymoon. I felt that because of all the obstacles we had overheard, we needed some time alone so we could work on our marriage. I also thought it would be a good time for my husband to meet my father, his wife, and several of my other family members on my mother's side, who also live in Georgia.

I suggested we stop in North Carolina first because I knew I couldn't drive all the way to Georgia in one night. My daughter's father wanted to meet my husband because I had discussed our marital problems with him over the phone since the time my husband and I got married.

Before leaving for our trip, I paid some of my debts and some of my husband's debts that he incurred before the marriage because I wanted our credit to be good when we got ready to purchase a home.

We left New Jersey on a Wednesday night at about ten

o'clock p.m. and headed for Wilmington, North Carolina. I drove nonstop for eight hours. My husband would pass me what I wanted to eat or drink, and he changed the music when we were tired of hearing the same songs.

On our way to North Carolina, I became very tired and sleepy, so I decided to pull over at a rest area about two hours away from Wilmington, North Carolina, to try and get a little sleep. As soon as I got comfortable, my husband pretended he was asleep and began snoring. He knew I couldn't sleep if I heard snoring noises. In more ways than one, my husband acted childish. I felt he didn't want me to sleep because he was so excited about getting to our destination. I knew I wasn't going to get any rest, so in anger, I started back down the highway, going almost 100 mph, trying to make my husband feel just as uncomfortable as I was. When I look back at what I did, I realize I could have killed us. I thank God for watching over me, even while I acted ignorantly.

After we arrived in North Carolina early Thursday morning, I phoned my daughter's father to tell him where we were so he could meet us and show us where we could get some breakfast and a hotel room. After my daughter's father met us, he asked my husband and me if we wanted to use one of his rooms at his house to rest. We turned down the offer because my husband said he would feel uncomfortable staying in his home.

While the three of us sat and ate breakfast, I looked at my daughter's father, and by the way he looked at me, I could tell he still had feelings for me. I have to admit I cared a lot about him, too, and I didn't want my husband to find out, so I tried not to make eye contact with my daughter's father while we ate.

After we were done eating, my husband and I followed my daughter's father to Market Street to a motel. My daughter's father made sure we were settled in, then he left. When we got into the motel room, I wasn't pleased with it because the room smelled of cigarette smoke, and the rooms weren't clean enough for me. When I went back to the office to see if I could get a nicer, non-smoking room, the lady at the front desk told me that was the only room she had left. I refused to stay in that room and decided to get my money back and try to find another motel. We went to several other motels that were on the same street, but the rooms were all run down, and the prices were too high. My husband and I decided it would be much cheaper if we stayed at my daughter's father's house, so I called him on the phone and asked him to come back so we could follow him to his house.

When we arrived, his niece was there, but his live-in girlfriend was at work. After saying hello to her, my husband and I went into the bedroom to lie down and get some rest. The room had twin beds in it. Because I was still mad at my husband, I slept in one bed, and he slept in another.

My husband came over to the bed I was in because he wanted to make love. It had been a long time since I had been sexually satisfied, so I decided to give him another chance and make love with him. My husband did the same thing he always did. He made sure he was satisfied and left me hanging. He claimed it was because we hadn't had sex for a long time, but I didn't want to hear that. Each time my husband failed to sexually satisfy me, I felt hurt, betrayed, unloved, and even angrier with him. I got out of bed and went into the bathroom, took a shower and left my husband in the room while I went to look for my daughter's father.

I was not thinking straight because I was so frustrated with my husband for being selfish and never sexually pleasing me. I knew my daughter's father still loved me, and I thought if I told him what my husband was doing to me sexually, he would be glad to do my husband's job for him. I thought if I had sex with my daughter's father, he would make sure I was sexually satisfied, and I would feel the love I was longing to feel.

When I came out of the room and found that my daughter's father wasn't home, I was very disappointed. I asked his niece where he had gone. She said she didn't know. I decided to go to his sister's house to look for him, but he wasn't there.

I sat and talked with my daughter's aunt about how I was feeling and how upset I was with my husband. I also told her the reason why I was looking for her brother. She laughed and said she knew I still loved her brother and that she would be happy to let us use her empty bedroom so we could have sex. After I sat and talked with my daughter's aunt for a while, I began to calm down, and I came to my senses. I changed my mind about wanting to sleep with my daughter's father because not only did I not want to sin against God, but I realized I didn't want to disrespect myself or my husband. Nor did I want to feel the guilt and shame of committing adultery.

When I went back to my former boyfriend's house, he had arrived. I sat in the dining room talking with him and his niece while my husband slept. I explained to my daughter's father that I needed to get some rest because I had a long way to drive. He suggested I drink some nighttime cough syrup to help me sleep. I drank the cough syrup, then went into the room to try to get some sleep.

As I lay in bed, thoughts of seeing my daughter's father with another woman made me sick. Even though I had taken the cough syrup, I still wasn't able to sleep. I didn't want to see my former boyfriend with another woman, so I figured it would be best if my husband and I left to find a hotel. We were going to Alpharetta, Georgia. My former boyfriend gave us directions on how to get there, and he said we could find a motel on the way, about an hour up the road.

When we came to the first motel, we stopped so I could get

some sleep. By this time, the cough syrup I had taken and the tiredness from driving all night had taken their toll on me.

When I went to the office to get the room, I made sure I got a room with twin beds in it because I didn't want to sleep in the same bed as my husband. I was frustrated, mad, and fed up with him for not sexually pleasing me.

After my husband and I got settled into our room, my husband tried to talk me into sleeping in the same bed with him, but I told him no because I was tired of him using me to please himself and not pleasing me. I told him I wasn't going to have sex with him anymore. He promised me he would satisfy me this time, but I didn't believe him. He had made that promise many times before and never kept it. I told him his sex wasn't any good and that I didn't want to have sex with him. I was very hurt, angry and frustrated so I turned over and I cried myself to sleep.

The following morning, we checked out of the motel and started back down the highway toward Georgia. We arrived at my uncle and aunt's house at about 12:00 p.m. No one was home because they were at work. We called ahead of time and informed them of the time we would be arriving, so they left the key under the doormat. My husband and I took showers, changed our clothes, and relaxed until my uncle and aunt came home.

I enjoyed our stay in Alpharetta, only because I got to spend time with my aunt and uncle. We also got to attend a church service at the church my aunt belonged to. The following weekend, my aunt took my husband and me to visit Martin Luther King's family home. We also visited the Martin Luther King Museum and the church he attended. My husband and I got through the day without arguing because we didn't want my aunt to know we weren't getting along. We put on a front when we were around my family members, but when we were alone or behind closed doors, we would argue. My husband and I slept in the same room, but we didn't sleep together. My husband slept in the bed, and I made a pallet and slept on the floor because I didn't want to sleep with him.

After visiting with my aunt and uncle for a couple of days, we then headed back down the highway to visit my father and his wife, who live in Valdosta, Georgia. My husband and I still weren't getting along, but we continued to act as if everything was all right. There really wasn't much to do in Valdosta, except visit my aunts and uncles on my father's side of the family. They mostly stayed to themselves, except for funerals, birthday parties, and family reunions.

We stayed with my father for a couple of days, but before we left my father went outside to check my van to make sure everything was all right. While my father checked my van, my husband was in the kitchen with me and my stepmother, talking about baking cakes. After my father was through checking my van, we said goodbye; then my husband and I packed our belongings in the van and headed back north for Myrtle Beach, South Carolina.

When we arrived in Myrtle Beach, I went into the hotel to get our room because I was the one who had the visa card. I booked a waterfront room because I thought it was very romantic, and I had always wanted to stay in one. The room had a king-size bed with a balcony so we could sit out and look at the water.

My husband and I got along long enough to walk along the beach and have a little fun at the amusement park. We even sat together to have our pictures hand-drawn at the amusement park, but when we went back to the room, we began to argue and fuss with each other. I thought if we stayed in a romantic waterfront room, it would help my husband and me have a romantic evening and make up, but it didn't. When we went to bed, I still didn't want him to touch me, so I ended up sleeping with my back turned to him the whole night. We stayed in Myrtle Beach, South Carolina, for one day and one night, and then we headed back to my former boyfriend's house in North Carolina. We stopped there, ate, and then headed back to New Jersey.

The trip was a disaster! I had to drive all the way because my husband didn't have a driver's license. I had to pump all the gas while my husband sat back and relaxed. Everywhere we went, we argued with one another. We didn't sleep together during the whole trip. If I wasn't doing something to try to hurt him, he was doing something to try to hurt me. We were worse off when we came home than we had been before we left.

I became stressed out and very depressed from everything that was going wrong in my marriage. After pleading with my husband and trying to get him to be the husband he promised he would to be to me I decided to seek the Lord about our marital problems. I prayed in times past about our marriage, but this time It was a desperate cry and prayer.

During prayer, God instructed me to have devotional service for about half an hour each night with my family. The Lord also instructed me to let each person have a chance to lead devotional service. The person in charge of devotional service had to sing a song, lead prayer, read a scripture, and give an exhortation on the scripture they read. When my husband began reading the scripture he had chosen, he read with hesitation, stumbling over most of the words because he didn't know them. My son sat in amazement, his mouth open wide in awe from the shock of realizing my husband couldn't read. I didn't want him to embarrass my husband, so I signaled to my son to stop acting out as we helped my husband pronounce the words he didn't know.

I knew my husband had trouble spelling, but I thought he

could read because every time I saw him, he was reading the Bible or the newspaper. However, after I heard him try to read, I realized my husband read at a lower grade level than both of my children who were twelve and thirteen at the time.

Finding out my husband couldn't read bothered me, but because I dropped out of school after completing the eighth grade, I understood and was willing to help him learn to read. It would have been better if my husband could have taken some reading classes, but because of his long hours at work, he couldn't. I, on the other hand, did go back to school to get my diploma. I haven't yet gotten it, but I do read at a college level, and in the classes I've already finished taking, I've gotten A's in all of them. I have all intentions of completing my education in the future.

I figured if my husband and I read the Bible together at night, that would be a good way for him to learn. My plan was to let him read, and when he came to words he couldn't pronounce, I would help him with them. But when I tried to help him, he would speak quickly over me before I could get the full pronunciation of the word out. It wasn't long before I realized that my husband's ego wouldn't allow him to let me help him.

A couple of weeks after finding out my husband couldn't read, the Lord revealed to me the lies my husband was telling me about why he didn't have his license.

My husband and I got into an argument about something, and he went to sleep on the couch. As I lay in bed, upset with my husband, the Lord spoke to me and told me to look in my husband's shaving bag that he used to carry his important papers in. I was never one to snoop into other people's things, so my first response was, "I'm not looking in his bag!" but the Lord insisted that I look. I opened the bag and looked; to my surprise, he had three permits in his bag. On each permit he had about seven failed stamps on them because he had taken the written part of the driving test and failed.

In New Jersey, once a person has taken the written part of the driver's test several times and failed, the person has to wait a year before he or she can take the test again. I realized then why my husband lied about not having his license and why he didn't make an effort to try to get his license after we were married, as he had promised. It was because he couldn't read so therefore he couldn't pass the written part of the test and after trying several times and failing he had to wait at least a year before he could take the test again.

I was upset with my husband for lying to me, and I let him know it, but I was determined to help him because I was tired of driving him around. I wanted him to drive me around sometimes. I also wanted to do everything in my power to try to make our marriage work.

I went to the Division of Motor Vehicles and asked if there was another way a person with a reading disability could take the test. The lady at the DMV told me he could take an oral test by having the questions read to him through headphones. I told my husband that after his year was up he could take the written part of the test orally, and he agreed to do so.

No matter what I did to try and make my marriage work, it continued to fall apart. My husband would always do something to provoke my anger. He wasn't pleasing me sexually. He came into the marriage lying, and he would not stand up for me to his family members. I believe my husband wanted me to constantly lash out at him to try and make me look like I had the problem when, in fact it was him who came into the marriage with lies and deceptions.

My husband continued to neglect me sexually. I became angrier and very frustrated with him, so I put him out of our bedroom. I gave my daughter's bedroom to him and put my daughter in my bedroom with me. I thought that by putting him out of our bedroom, I would teach him a lesson and he would make up his mind to start satisfying me sexually, but it only caused us to argue more, and we grew further apart.

I didn't know what else to do, so I began to pray, but to my surprise, God began to deal with me for putting Him out of our bedroom. After I asked the Lord to forgive me for putting my husband out of our bedroom, I asked God to intervene on my behalf. God instructed me to go to my husband and apologize to him for putting him out of our room.

I obeyed God, and I went to my husband with tears in my eyes and apologized for putting him out of our bedroom. I explained to him how I felt about him not satisfying me sexually and how he didn't stick up for me to his family members. My husband promised me he would do his best to satisfy me sexually and that he would defend me to his family members when necessary. The following day while he was at work and the kids were at school I put his things back in our bedroom and put my daughter's things back in her bedroom.

I always did my wifely duties. I kept the house clean; I made sure my husband's dinner was ready for him when he came home from work. I made sure his clothes were washed, hung, neatly folded, and put away, but my husband continued to neglect me. I found myself even more frustrated, stressed out, and depressed, and the marriage had taken a toll on my kids' emotional state. My kids felt I loved my husband more than them. They began to feel neglected and started having feelings of dislike for my husband.

Even though God revealed to me the secrets my husband was keeping from me, I still wanted my marriage to work, but it seemed like the more I tried, the worse things got. I didn't feel like my husband loved me because I never received affection from him. I also felt like he loved his family more than me. I was at the end of my rope, so I figured it would be a good idea for my husband and me to take a break from each other. I told my husband to go stay with his sister and daughter for awhile until he could figure out what he wanted to do about our marriage.

My husband didn't take all of his belongings when he left because we had every intention of getting back together, but after my husband didn't call for several days I became very upset and I didn't want any of my husband's belongings in my apartment. I gathered all his belongings and started to pile them up by the door, but as I began piling his belongings by the door the Lord spoke to me and told me to pack his things together nice and neat. I obeyed God and repacked his things nice and neat. I cut small wholes in each plastic bag big enough for the top of the hanger to fit in then I slid my husband's clothes in the bag and tied the end of the bags so his clothes wouldn't fall out or get wrinkled.

My husband had coats stored in my son's closet. When I took his coat out of the closet and laid it on the couch to put it in a plastic bag, the Lord spoke to me again and told me to look in his coat pocket. I was hesitant at first because, as I said before, I don't like snooping in other people's things, but the Lord insisted that I look in his pocket, so I did, and to my surprise, I came across the paycheck stubs he claimed his job didn't give him for working during the summer months. I was furious because my husband had lied to me again. I kept the paycheck stubs for proof.

When my husband and his friend came to my apartment, they were surprised to see all his belongings packed up and waiting at the door for him. I told my husband to get his things and not come back, and if anyone asked him why our marriage didn't work, I told him to tell them it was because he was a liar. Then I showed him the paycheck stub from his pocket.

Having my husband out of my apartment was as if a big weight had lifted off me, and my children were happy he was gone as well. After my husband left the house, I began to experience the peace I had before he came to live with us. I had bills that needed paying, but that was okay because God had made sure my bills were paid in times past, and I knew He would continue to provide for me.

When I called my Section Eight worker to let her know my husband had moved out, she told me that she had not gotten around to adjusting my rent. That was a blessing because if she had adjusted my rent, it would have gone from one hundred seventy-six dollars to about one thousand dollars, and I would have had to come up with the money until she could adjust it back to what I was paying before my husband came to live with me.

My husband called several times, but not once did he ask me if I needed anything. I felt in my spirit that he thought because I wasn't working, I was going to ask him to come back home because I couldn't pay the bills. I could have used his help, but I wasn't going to let him know it. I was able to use my hair-braiding talent that God blessed me with to pay my bills.

In my opinion, a man who loves his wife would have made sure she was all right, even though they were separated, especially if he had plans to reconcile with her.

After being separated for several weeks, my husband and I decided to meet at my apartment and try to work things out over dinner. I made fried whiting fish, fried shrimp with French fries, and, for dessert, I baked a cake.

While my husband and I sat at the kitchen table, the Lord spoke to me and told me not to say too much. He told me to listen to what my husband had to say. The whole time my husband talked, he talked about everything but us. As he talked, tears began to run down my face, and it was at that point that I realized he didn't have a clue how to be a husband to me.

I got up from the table because now I wanted to just go to my room and be alone. I didn't want to hear anything else he had to say. Because it was late, I told my husband he could sleep on the couch. I gave him a pillow and a cover, then I went into my bedroom. My husband followed me into my bedroom and insisted that he was sorry for hurting me.

What he talked about next was really unbelievable. He talked about what he had done for his daughter and how much money he had given her. I was very hurt, angry, and I felt betrayed. I wasn't upset with him for doing for his daughter. I was his wife, and he knew my financial situation, and not once did he ask me if I needed anything; yet he could sit in my face and talk about all that he had done for his daughter.

It was at this point that I made up my mind that the marriage was over. I told my husband to please get out of my room and leave me alone. When he went into the living room, I shut and locked my bedroom door. He tried several times to get me to open my bedroom door so he could talk to me, but I would not open it.

About an hour later, I took off my wedding rings, brought them into the living room, and gave them back to him because they didn't have any meaning to me anymore, so I didn't want them. When I got up the next morning, my husband was gone, and he had taken my wedding ring with him, and I didn't see him anymore after that.

Leave your kindred and friends!

Not long after my husband and I separated, I received a call from my attorney asking me how "thirty-two thousand dollars" sounded. I told him it sounded good. He then told me I should be getting my settlement in a couple of weeks for the injuries I received from the car accident I was in two years prior. I was surprised at the news because, prior to hearing this, my lawyer had told me I wouldn't receive my settlement until the following year.

After receiving my settlement, I gave ten percent tithes and an offering to the church my mother attended. Then, I paid off most of my credit card debts, and I planned a vacation to visit my father and his wife in Valdosta, Georgia. I told my father why my marriage had ended and he told me he knew my marriage wasn't going last because he saw my husband as being a wimp because he was more interested in cooking than working with my father while he tried to make sure the car was alright for the drive back home.

While I was driving to Valdosta, Georgia, to visit my father, God began dealing with me about moving to the South. After my nephew, my daughter, and my daughter's friend arrived at my father's house, I discussed the possibility of us moving to Valdosta, Georgia, to be around my father. My father's wife and I even went around looking and gathering information on the prices and sizes of mobile homes.

After leaving my father's home, I took my children to visit my daughter's father in Wilmington, North Carolina. During the ride from Valdosta, Georgia, to Wilmington, North Carolina, my children expressed their dislike for Valdosta, Georgia. They said they didn't want to live there because it was boring. I took what they said into consideration because they were right.

After arriving at my daughter's father's house, my daughter told me she wouldn't mind moving to North Carolina. I figured if I let my children choose where we moved, they would be happy about the move, so I decided to take my daughter's suggestion into consideration about moving to North Carolina; that way, she could be near her father. I made arrangements with my daughter's aunt for me to come back to North Carolina and stay with her for a week while I looked for a place to live.

After I arrived back in New Jersey, I thought about the idea of moving constantly. I was hesitant about moving to North Carolina because I knew I still had feelings for my daughter's father, and I didn't want to set myself up to fall into adultery with him. I also wanted to make sure moving to North Carolina was the Lord's will for my life. I prayed about the situation and expressed to God my feelings for my daughter's father. The Lord gave me the go ahead to move, but instructed me to stay away from my daughter's father.

My son and I drove back to North Carolina to my daughter's aunt's house, where we stayed for a week while I looked for a place to live. My daughter's aunt's husband had to work, so I asked my daughter's father to go around with me to show me how to get to the different apartment complexes and houses that were up for rent.

We went to this one house that was for rent off of Market Street. The inside of the house was being redone, but the outside was a mess. I didn't like the place, and neither did my son. This apartment was a step down from what we were used to. We had gotten used to living in a nice environment and in a nice apartment. My daughter's father said, "If I were you, I would jump on it." I turned to him and asked him if his house looked like this house. From past experiences with my daughter's father, I've seen him pick out things that weren't up to par for someone else, but if it was for him, it was nice. I turned down the house and decided to stop looking for the day.

When my daughter's uncle came home from work, I explained to him the condition of the house and where the house was that my daughter's father told me I should take. He explained to me about the area and told me he was glad I didn't take the house. Since he knew Wilmington well, he told me he had a good idea of where I should move. He and I went to the store and got a newspaper and a book with lists of houses that were available for rent. After getting back to his house, he and I sat down at the kitchen table to look through the newspaper and apartment book for available houses for rent. He told me to circle everything that said "North Chase." I called out available houses, and he told me whether they were in a nice area or not. I then called each landlord and made arrangements to meet with them to see the houses.

One gentleman I spoke with had two houses for rent. One house, he said, someone was already interested in renting, but he said we could look at the other mobile home he had for rent. The next day, we went to look at the mobile home. I didn't like the way the outside of the house looked, so I crossed it off my list. Out of curiosity, we drove by the other house he had for rent to see what it looked like. It was in North Chase, which is a nice neighborhood, and from the looks of the outside of the house, it was very nice. I wanted to see what the inside looked like, so I called the landlord and asked him if we could see the inside of the house, even though he had said someone was already interested in renting it. The landlord was very nice. He said, "Sure, meet me at the house in five minutes." As soon as I walked into the house, I knew it was the house for me. My furniture coordinated with the house. There were three large bedrooms and two full bathrooms. One bathroom was in the master bedroom. The master bedroom had a walk-in closet, and the closets in each of the other rooms had a lot of space.

I told the landlord I wanted the house and I was ready to write him out a check for two months in advance and a month and a half security deposit. There's this saying money talks. Well this was one of the times money talked. The landlord agreed to rent me the house. I also told him I was on the section eight programs and asked him if he was willing to rent to a section eight tenant. Since he didn't know about the program I had to explain it to him. He said he would give the program a try. I also told him the money wasn't in my checking account, but it was in my saving account and if he would hold off cashing the check until I returned to New Jersey to transfer the money from my savings account into my checking account and he said yes.

When I arrived back home I planned on waiting until the following day to transfer the money from my savings account into my checking account, but the Lord instructed me to do it as soon as I arrived in New Jersey. Out of obedience, I went directly to the bank and transferred the money. I'm glad I did what the Lord instructed me to do because the landlord did not waste any time cashing the check. The following day, I went to my bank to check my account balance. I found out the landlord cashed the check at a Wachovia branch in North Carolina. My landlord cashed the check right away because he wanted to make sure the check was good before he took the house off the market.

I gave my building complex secretary a sixty day notice of my plans to move out. During the sixty days, I packed my things and made arrangements for a moving company to come into my apartment to give me an estimate of what it would cost to move my things from New Jersey to Wilmington, North Carolina. The movers gave me an estimate of two thousand dollars with free storage for a month. I made it known to the movers that I didn't want any surprise costs on the day they came to move my belongings and they assured me there would be no surprise costs.

During the last two months I lived in New Jersey, I didn't belong to any church because I didn't want to join another church after leaving my last church. I had lost all trust in Christians and pastors because of how my former pastors and fellow brothers and sisters in the Lord treated me, but I loved God, and I wanted to continue to worship Him, so I visited churches. I didn't try to get involved with any ministry, nor did I want to get close to anyone in the churches. All I did was go to church, worship God, and leave just before church was over to avoid getting close to anyone. I figured if I did this, no one could get close to me to hurt me.

When the movers came to put my belongings on the truck, they told me I had more boxes than they expected, so I would have to pay an additional six hundred dollars for them to move my things. When the movers said this, they had already started packing my things onto the truck. I told my brother and my nephews to take all my belongings off the truck because I wasn't paying the extra money. The movers got nervous and called their boss, and their boss told them to move my things for the estimated price that was quoted to me. The movers ended up taking everything I owned, even things that weren't supposed to go on the truck, and they also gave me extra boxes for free.

After all my things were on the truck, I went to the bank to withdraw money to carry with me. While I was waiting in line, my beautician came into the bank. She had been telling me that she had a friend who lived in Wilmington, North Carolina, and she wanted to give me her number so I would have a contact when I arrived in North Carolina, but it would slip our minds each time we were together. This time she made sure she gave me her friend's name and number and she told me to make sure I give her a call when I arrived in North Carolina.

My sister and I followed one another in separate cars to North Carolina. She stopped at my house for a little rest, then she headed down the road to Columbus, Georgia.

My children and I slept on an air mattress because my furniture wasn't set to arrive for another week or so. I brought my small television with a VCR with us in the car so we could at least watch some VCR tapes since the cable was not yet hooked up. I also brought a few pots, silverware, and dishes to cook with, along with several other items we needed.

Be Offended? I Don't Think So!

After the truck delivered my furniture and the rest of my belongings, I unpacked my things and got settled in. I had the cable turned on and the telephone service activated. I chose my garbage company. I enrolled the kids in school. Everything was going well until I decided I needed to find a church home. I was reluctant to look for a church home because of my past experiences at the churches in New Jersey, so I decided I would take my time finding one.

Even though I decided to take my time finding a church home, the devil wasn't taking his time doing his job. All of a sudden, I became very homesick, lonely, and depressed. I started to regret moving to North Carolina. I remember saying, "Oh my God, what have I done?" This was the first time I had ever done something this drastic in my life. I moved my children and all of my belongings far away from my family, friends, and my familiar environment.

The more I thought about being away from my family and friends, the more depressed I became. All I wanted to do was eat and sleep so I wouldn't have to think about being away from home or feel the sensation of being alone and bored. I gained weight; I went from wearing a size fourteen to a size eighteen. Gaining weight made me feel even more depressed and frustrated.

Before I left New Jersey, a minister looked up apostolic churches on the internet and gave them to me. I knew I had to get out and meet saved people, so I looked at the list and chose a church located on Fourth Street. I drove to the church on Saturday to make sure I could find it on Sunday morning. My children and I went to church there on Sunday morning. I didn't like the church because it reminded me of the apostolic churches I had attended in New Jersey. The church smelled of mildew. There weren't many members, and my kids didn't like the church. I didn't want to get caught up in another apostolic church, so I decided not to go back to that church.

During the week, as I sat on my bed and thought about where I should go to church, the Lord reminded me of the phone number my beautician in New Jersey had given me, and He laid it on my heart to call the lady to find out where the church was that she attended. After calling the lady and speaking with her, she gave me directions to her house so I could meet her and follow her to church on Sunday.

The following Sunday, when I visited the church, I knew this was the church where God wanted me, but I wanted to be sure, so I didn't join. I figured I would go a couple more times before my children and I joined. The third time attending the church, I decided to join. My daughter said she didn't like the church, but I didn't pay her any mind because this was a natural response for her. My son said he liked the church. I listen to my children's likes and dislikes, but when it all boils down God has the last say.

Even though I would pray and attend church regularly I still felt bound with feeling lonely, depressed and with being homesick. One Sunday Bishop Richburg stood in front of the church waving a handkerchief and said "the devil has unleashed legions of demons against this person but no weapon formed will prosper". I listened to what the Bishop said, but I had no idea he was talking about me. The Bishop walked up the isle and stopped at the end of the pew I was sitting on and threw the handkerchief. Without thinking I caught it. When I caught it Bishop shook his head saying "uh hmm!" I want you to take this handkerchief and wave it around your house and plead the blood of Jesus and when you do the devil is going to flee. I knew what he said was true because I knew what I was going through was an attack of the enemy.

After church, when I arrived home I did what the Bishop told me to do. I told my children to wait outside while I went into the house, waved the handkerchief around, and pleaded the blood of Jesus. Immediately, the depression left and a spirit of peace was in me and my home. I thank God for deliverance!

I always worked in the churches I attended, but because I had been hurt by members and pastors, I was happy just attending church services and going home. I didn't trust anyone, and I didn't want to get too close to anyone, especially the pastor. I wanted to go to church, praise the Lord, and then go home, but God had other plans for me.

I remember Bishop getting up and saying, "I know you are a worker, and we're going to find something for you to do." Even though I was reluctant to work, I just shook my head, okay, hoping he would forget all about putting me to work, but that didn't happen.

One Sunday, Bishop got up and announced that God told him to put me over the youth department. I didn't want to do it, but I knew I had to be obedient and do what God wanted me to do. I knew God told him to put me over the youth department because God had anointed me to work with children and I had worked with the children in the other churches.

As soon as Bishop announced that God told him to put me over the youth department, the enemy started attacking me through people. All of a sudden, others in the church felt they should be the ones to work with the youth. They even went as far as getting up during the church service and announcing that they were the ones working with the youth. The pastor's wife stood up boldly and told everyone that the Bishop put her over the youth and that if they wanted to work with her, they should help in whatever way possible. But I was the youth director. Even though I realized what the enemy was doing, I didn't say anything. I did wonder why, all of a sudden, they wanted to work with the youth when they had their chance before I came along.

The devil knew God was going to do mighty things in the youth department, so he did everything he could to stop the youth department from going forth. The Lord told me to choose the same person who wanted to be over the youth to be the assistant youth director. I didn't understand why God had me choose her, but I was always one who tried to obey God even when I didn't understand what He was doing.

I wanted God to be in control of the youth department, so I would get up early in the morning, about two o'clock a.m., to pray for the youth department. God began giving me specific direction about how to run the youth department. Every fourth Sunday, the youth department was in charge of the service, but God was in control. The Spirit of God would move in a mighty way on every fourth Sunday.

I still wasn't trying to get close to anyone in the church because I held unforgiveness in my heart toward church people, and I didn't trust them. Even though God was using me in the youth department, I still found myself slipping backward because I had unforgiveness in my heart. I found myself looking for love and approval from an unsaved man. I found myself in an ungodly relationship, committing fornication and being comfortable in it.

I was raised in an Apostolic Church with very strict rules. One rule was that a member could not be active in any church ministry if he or she was not living right. At another church I attended, the person was made to sit on the back pew. I am one who doesn't play with God. I felt that because I wasn't living right, I had no business being the youth director. I asked my bishop if he would sit me down from being the youth leader because I wasn't living right. The pastor asked me if I loved him. I said yes because I thought I did. He also asked me if he loved me. I said I didn't know; I thought he did. Then he asked me if he wanted to marry me. I said no. The Bishop then told me one thing I had was the fear of God, which was a good sign. The Bishop stood thinking for about a minute, then he told me he didn't want to sit me down right then because he didn't want me to get comfortable with the way I was living and back slide. He told me to keep working with the youth and he was going to pray about the situation and if God told him to sit me down he would. I was somewhat disappointed because I didn't feel worthy to work with the youth while committing fornication. Nor would I dare partake of communion on first Sundays.

I decided that since the pastor wouldn't sit me down from being the youth director, I would run the youth department from the sidelines. I appointed teenage children who were part of the youth department to lead the service and other church members to pray for the children as I stood for prayer with them for myself.

When the youth couldn't come to rehearsal on Saturdays, I would get up early on Sunday mornings, go to South Port, pick them up and meet the other youth at the church to have choir rehearsal. The kids were willing to sacrifice getting up early in the morning for choir rehearsal because they were excited about singing.

I wasn't living right, but God would still speak to me and tell me which person to have doing which job on Youth Sunday. As I sat in the pew each Youth Sunday, I would watch the Spirit of God show up and move in a mighty way. I realized that, in spite of me, God still got the glory, and I had nothing to do with it.

I made it known to the other youth directors that I needed help, but instead of working with me, they criticized what I was doing. I even made announcements before the whole church asking for help with the youth, but the more I asked for help, the less I received. I admit I didn't do everything right, but instead of working with me, they focused on my mistakes and held them against me. One reason was that the devil didn't want me in charge of the youth department, and they allowed the devil to use them to work against me. Because I wasn't spiritually mature, I allowed the enemy to win.

One day, I sat at my desk assigning duties for the youth as God gave them to me. Then, I called them to make them aware of the jobs they were assigned to do, as I always did. God laid it on my heart to rotate the duties so every youth could participate and be trained in leading the service on Youth Sunday. One day, I called the youth secretary, and we ended up getting into an argument over the phone. We ended up saying things to each other that we shouldn't have said.

I decided to call the other youth director to find out if she had any concerns about the youth department. She assured me everything was all right between her and me concerning the youth department. I also felt in my heart that the other members in the youth department wanted me out so the assistant youth director could have my position.

Because of the disagreement between the youth secretary and me, complaints were made to the pastor. I, too, had some concerns with the other leaders of the youth department about not getting the help I needed from them. The pastor and the assistant pastor had a meeting with the youth leaders to try to resolve the problems we were having.

In the meeting, the pastor told everyone that if we had any issues, now was the time to make them known. I already knew the youth secretary and I had issues because of the argument we had over the phone. After she and I expressed how we felt, it was necessary for us to apologize to each other for what we had said to one another.

When the pastor asked the assistant youth director if she had any concerns about the way the youth department was being run, to my surprise, she said yes. I was somewhat shocked because when I called her and asked her if she had any concerns about the way I was running things, she told me no.

She expressed that she didn't like the idea of me going around and openly stating I needed help with the youth department. I only did this because she and the other youth leaders refused to help me with the youth. I felt they were not helping because they wanted to make my job as hard as possible. If they really wanted to help, they would have come to me and asked what needed to be done, but they didn't. They acted as if I had never asked for help or didn't need help.

As I listened to what the other youth leaders said in the meeting, I realized my instincts were right. They were against me, and they were also trying to make me look bad because they wanted the assistant youth director to have my position.

I felt that if they were willing to stoop so low to get my position, I figured I would give them what they wanted, so I quit. Not only did I quit being the youth leader, but I also decided to leave the church. This is the way I always reacted when the devil would use someone in the church to work against me. It was more comfortable for me to run than to stay and endure hardship like a good soldier.

Not only was I upset with the youth leaders for working against me, but I was somewhat shocked, disappointed, and upset with the pastor because he insisted they didn't want my position, even after I told him their motives for working and talking against me. The bottom line was they wanted me out so the assistant youth director could have my position.

Even though I felt disappointed in the pastor, I didn't hold it against him, and I kept in contact with him after I left the church. I realize the devil can be sneaky and cunning when he is working through people, especially when he works through my brothers and sisters in the Lord.

My pastor was the only person I kept in contact with from the church. Even the one person I confided in and took counsel from stopped calling me. In my heart, I felt there were some members of the church who were glad I left, but there were some who missed me. I felt hurt, betrayed, and I felt that no one loved me because none of the members from the church called to check on me.

I didn't want to pray about leaving the church because I felt that if I prayed, God would show me my faults and then tell me to go back to the church and apologize. I wanted to continue to feel the way I felt so I could justify my actions for leaving the church.

My children and I didn't attend any church service for a couple of weeks because I didn't know which church to attend. After several weeks of not going to church, I spoke with my neighbor, and she invited us to visit the church she attended. The following Sunday, my children and I went to church with her. The worship was awesome, but the morning service only lasted for two hours; then we went home for the rest of the day. I wasn't used to that. In the service I felt I was lost in the crowd and out of place, but I continued to go until God began to deal with me.

The first thing God allowed me to realize was that He didn't allow the members to call me because He wanted to minister to me, and He didn't want anybody to interfere with my spiritual growth and process.

The next thing God had me do was to read "The Bait of Satan" by John Bevere. The book talked about being offended and forgiveness. As I read the book, I began to realize I was harboring years of unforgiveness in my heart. I had to forgive all the people who had hurt me, from New Jersey to North Carolina: my ex-husband, two of my ex-pastors, the youth leaders at the church I had just left and other members who I knew didn't like me.

Along with God's instructions to read the "Bait of Satan," He also instructed me to go on a fruit and vegetable fast for seven days. He instructed me to wear dresses or skirts for seven days as I fasted. He instructed me not to go to Leland, not to talk a lot on the phone, and to watch the movie "The Passion of the Christ" by Mel Gibson. The movie helped me remember what Christ went through leading up to His crucifixion, during His crucifixion, and how His love for us led Him to forgive and pray for the very same people who crucified Him. He prayed, "Father, forgive them, for they know not what they do." If Christ could forgive after all He went through, who was I not to forgive? After I watched the movie, I began to weep. I went into my secret closet and prayed. I repented for having unforgiveness toward all the people who had offended me. I forgave everyone whom I had allowed to offend me, and then I asked the Lord to forgive me.

It wasn't long before the Lord began to deal with me about the ungodly relationship I was in with the man from New Jersey. Before I go on, I would like to give you some background on why I allowed myself to get involved with him and other men prior to him.

When a man gave me things it made me feel loved and it would comfort me when others would hurt me. Every time someone would hurt me or I would feel rejected I would get into a relationship with a man to make me feel better.

Getting into relationships with men made me feel better for a little while; then the Spirit of the Lord would convict me so strongly that I would begin to feel bad. I would repent, but as soon as the guilt was gone, I would turn around and commit fornication with him again. Eventually, I became comfortable in the relationship even though I vowed to serve God for the rest of my life. At times, I would openly express to the man that I wasn't living right and that I was wrong for having sex with him. He wasn't saved, so he didn't pay what I said any attention.

I loved God, and I wanted to stop sinning against Him, but I was caught up with what the man was doing for me. He would take me to the finest restaurants. Whenever I needed money, he would give me a couple of hundred dollars at a time. He would deposit money into my bank account at the branch in New Jersey, which made it easier for me to travel back and forth from North Carolina to New Jersey to visit him. While I was in NJ, he would pay for my hotel room for however long I planned to stay there. He brought me gold chains, earrings, and a diamond bracelet. On Christmas, he brought my children what they wanted. I completely stopped trusting in God and began depending on the man to give me what I needed and wanted.

During my seven-day fast, God began reminding me where

He brought me from and how He had healed my body of the HIV virus. God also reminded me how I would die if I continued in the state I was in. I decided that what the man had to offer me wasn't worth dying and going to hell for, so I made up my mind to leave him alone while I still had a chance. Not only was the relationship sinful, but the man had another woman in NJ, and I was tired of feeling hurt every time he was with her.

I called the man and told him I had to leave him alone and the reason why. He said he was coming to North Carolina, so I figured we would talk about it more when he got here. This would be the last time I would see him, but the man had other plans on his mind. He thought if he brought me the "1 ct. diamond bracelet" I wanted, I would change my mind about leaving him, but I didn't. I took the bracelet and still decided not to see him anymore. After the man went back to New Jersey, I stopped calling him and asking him for money. I had to break all ties with him until I was strong enough in spirit to speak to him.

I was in Wal-Mart looking at the Christian books. One of the children picked up a book titled "Matters of the Heart" by Juanita Bynum and stated that her mother read the book. She also said her mother said the book was good. The girl handed me the book, and I decided to read the back of it to see what it was about. After reading the back of the book, I decided to purchase the book so I could read the entire thing.

The book "Matters of the Heart" talks about being backslidden from the heart and receiving a new heart—the new heart God gave me when I first got saved. The new heart that loved God and people so much that there was nothing anyone could do to offend me.

I allowed myself to be offended, and I committed fornication time after time. I realized I had backslidden in my heart, and I needed a new heart. Above everything, I desired and needed a heart that pleases God.

After reading a portion of the book, I decided I needed to pray. As I prayed, I repented and asked the Lord to create in me a clean heart and renew within me a right spirit. Immediately, God began to cleanse and purge me. All the towels I used during my purging, God told me to throw away. He would bless me with more towels.

God began to minister to me. He told me I was delivered from the man I sinned with from New Jersey. He said the man's spirit no longer dwelt within me. While God ministered to me, I danced all over my bedroom. God had washed me, cleansed me, and purged me. I wasn't the same. I didn't think the same, nor did I act the same. God had saved me all over again, and it felt good!

After God purged me and gave me a new heart, He began to minister to me about going back to Salvation and Deliverance Church. He told me to go back to the church, and whatever the pastor told me to do concerning the ministry, to do it. God told me He would be with me and not to mind the people. He told me to keep my eyes on Him by fasting, praying, and reading His Word.

As soon as God was done ministering to me, I called Pastor Richburg and told him God wanted me to come back to the church. Pastor Richburg replied, "You know you are welcome, and there is always room for you at the church."

The following Wednesday, I went to Bible study, and on Sunday, I went to church. I returned with a different mindset, a heart filled with love for every member of the church, and a deeper desire to work for the Lord.

It wasn't long after I went back to Salvation and Deliverance when we started our yearly Daniels twenty-one day Daniels fast. During the fast God began to minister to me about preaching. During my prayer time in my secret closet I was slain in the Spirit by the power of God as God began to tell me he was anointing me to preach the gospel, to lay hands on the sick and they would recover.

God told me I'm blessed. He said I am part of the chosen remnant. He said men shall see and know that I am called by Him. He told me not to worry about what others say about me and not to worry about how they look at me. God told me my heart has found favor with Him. He said when I open my mouth, wisdom and knowledge will come forth that only God gives. People will hear, see, and know I am delivered. God told me I would no longer struggle to walk upright before Him. God told me He has made me to sit amongst kings and princes. I felt unworthy as I wept. God encouraged me by telling me that because people said I wasn't going to be anything, He was going to show forth His glory through my life. I replied to God by saying, "O.K., God, You anointed me to preach, so You will have to reveal it to the pastor." I decided in my heart not to say anything to my pastor until God revealed it to him.

After this awesome encounter with God, I continued to feel the presence of the Lord so strongly during each church service. It wasn't long until God revealed to my pastor that He had called me to preach.

One Sunday after service, my pastor came to me and told me he had his eye on me. Hearing him say that made me realize God had revealed to him that He called me to preach, but I still wasn't going to say anything until he said something to me first. A few days later, Pastor Richburg came to me and told me he was waiting on me. I replied by telling him I was waiting on him. It wasn't long after that Pastor Richburg, along with his wife, called me into his office and asked me what was going on. I knew he was talking about God calling me to preach, so I confirmed to him that God had indeed called me to preach.

Pastor Richburg then told me he wanted me to get with his wife, Evangelist Richburg, to go over what was expected of me as an evangelist. As Evangelist Richburg stood listening, I expressed to her that I didn't want to preach because I knew that by accepting the call to preach, I would have to endure many trials and tribulations. However, even though I felt this way, I knew I had to be obedient to the will of God. Pastor Richburg then told me he wanted me to give him a date when I wanted to do my initial sermon. I asked him if I could give it to him after the fast because I had to pray and see when God wanted me to do it and what He wanted me to preach.

A couple of days after meeting with the pastor the Lord gave me the 20th of March 2006 to do my initial sermon and two days before our Daniels fast was to be over, God gave me my sermon. The title was "Be offended I don't think so!" my text was taken from St. Luke 17:1-4; 14:27 and Hebrews 4: 15-16.

Overcoming and Doing the Will of God

A couple of weeks after accepting the call to preach, I received an attack from the devil. I began to experience severe back pains. The pains were so severe that the doctor had to change my medication. The doctor prescribed 25 milligrams of Duragesic patches. I was instructed to wear the patch at all times and to change it every three hours. The Duragesic patch is given to people who have lifelong injuries with constant pain and to people who are terminally ill with incurable diseases. After wearing the patch for a couple of weeks, I realized it wasn't strong enough. It wasn't lasting three days, so I had to change it before the third day. The doctor changed my prescription from 25 milligrams to 50 milligrams.

Wearing the patches helped my pain, but it caused me to nod out all the time. I didn't want to go anywhere; I just wanted to stay in my bed. The only places I would go were to church and to the store. My kids even said, "Mommy, all you do is stay in your room watching television. You never go anywhere or do anything."

While I was at church attending our church anniversary, I

almost overdosed on the medicine from the patch because I was doing a lot of moving as I praised the Lord. Each time I moved my arm, medicine was going into my system. The church was very hot and crowded, so I began to feel very faint and nauseated. I knew I was feeling this way from the patch, so I went into the Sunday school room and took the patch off and then I went back into the sanctuary and continued to praise the Lord.

Everyone in the sanctuary was asked to stand, but I couldn't because too much medicine had already gotten into my system, causing me to feel very hot and faint as I was going to pass out. One of the sisters realized something was wrong with me so she and a couple of other sisters began to fan me. After they fanned me for a little while they realized I was about to faint so they took me into another room where it was cooler and gave me some water to drink, while another sister rubbed my face with a cool paper towel.

I began to feel somewhat better, but one of the sisters told me I still looked pale, and when I looked at the palm of my right hand it had turned purple. I began to feel nausea as if I had to vomit so I went into the bathroom, leaned over the toilet and I began to vomit up dark yellow, very bitter stuff. After I finished vomiting I felt much, better so I went back into the Sunday school room and sat down.

I didn't want to go back into the church because I thought I would pass out from the heat, but Pastor Richburg told one of the sisters to bring me back into the church so he could pray for me. As I entered the church I began to feel faint again. As I was trying to make my way toward the front of the church I began to feel as though I was going to pass out. As I approached my pastor, I went to reach for him for support to keep from falling.

The visiting pastor began to pray and command a foul

spirit to come out of me, but Pastor Richburg told the ladies to seat me down on the pew and give me some water to drink. Then my Pastor made it know to the visiting Pastor that I was getting an attack from the enemy because I was about to do my initial sermon. The visiting Pastor's wife held me close to her as she prayed and I began to feel totally better.

When I went home that night the Lord spoke to me and told me not to put the duragesic pain patch back on. I obeyed God and I was determined not to put the patch back on. That night I went to bed without the patch. The following day when I woke up I realized I was going through withdrawal. I was so sick all I could do is lay in the bed and sleep. I slept for twenty-four hours straight and while I was asleep I had a dream I was pulling yellow stuff out of my mouth.

When I did wake up I felt like I was going to die. I was experiencing hot sweats, vomiting, diarrhea, my body was weak and I couldn't eat anything and as I laid in bed I couldn't think straight. I felt as if I was about to lose my mind, but in the midst of it all I remembered the dream I had while I was asleep and I could hear church music playing in my mind. Hearing the church music helped me to realize God was with me.

My kids went on with their lives because they thought I was just sleeping like I always did. They didn't know what I was going through and how sick I was.

When I did get enough strength to get out of bed I was feeling so bad I decided to call the paramedic so they could take me to the hospital. The paramedics took so long coming I decided to call my pastor to tell him what I was going through. Pastor Richburg asked me did I need to go to the hospital. I told him yes and he said he would be right over to take me.

Before Pastor Richburg could get to my house the paramedics came. I explained to them I had taken off the duragesic patch and I was going through withdrawal, but after they found out my medical history they insisted I was sick with the flu or a virus because of my HIV history. I reassured them God had healed me of the HIV virus and that wasn't the cause of me being sick. I realized the paramedics were set on the HIV virus causing my illness and not the withdrawal symptoms, so I told them I didn't want them to take me to the hospital. I was going to wait for my pastor and let him take me.

After my pastor arrived at my home he waited patiently as I prepared myself to go to the hospital. On the way to the hospital I expressed to my Pastor I was hot and then cold. He replied with a joke and told me I wasn't sick I was just going through menopause. The way he said it was funny, so I began to laugh even though I was feeling bad. I thank God I waited for my pastor to take me to the hospital because he made me feel better when he made me laugh and I was able to take my focus off the way I was really feeling. My pastor had me laughing all the way to the hospital and while we waited in the waiting room at the hospital.

A man walked up to us and said hello as if he knew us and out of love, respect and courtesy we spoke back. When the man walked off Pastor looked at me and asked me did I know the man? I replied by saying "I don't know the man, do you?" He said, "I don't know the man either" and we both laughed.

I thank God for my pastor because he taught me what a true pastor is. He is concerned about all his members' well-being. He continually lifts us up in prayer and he treats us with love, care and compassion. He allows God to use him and he is not so saved that he doesn't take time out to have fun.

My pastor could not stay the whole time with me at the hospital, so he called one of the evangelists to come stay with me. When she walked into my hospital room I was crying because of the way I felt. I immediately asked her did everyone who was called to preach have to go through this. She told me yes, and then she explained to me what she went through when she got ready to do her initial sermon.

When the doctor came into the room I explained to him that I had taken off my duragesic patch. The doctor was very upset because he said I shouldn't have taken off the patch. I was supposed to be weaned off them. I told the doctor the Lord told me to take off the patch and I would lay here and die before I put them back on. The doctor told me since my mind was made up not to put the patches back on the only thing he could do was to give me something to ease the withdrawal symptoms. He gave me two shots that helped me feel a little better than sent me home.

When I went into my house I felt paranoid and as if the house was going to close in on me, so I ran next door to the neighbors house and wept on her shoulders. I asked her if I could sit and talk with her until I calmed down. After sitting and talking with her for about a half an hour I felt a little better.

When I went back to my home I tried to force myself to stay home, but I couldn't because I still felt like the house was closing in on me. I decided to get in my car and go for a drive. I was in no shape to drive, but I just couldn't stay home alone.

As I was driving down the highway I decided to call a mother who attended the same church as me. I tried to explain to her what I was going through. I even told her I felt the devil was trying to kill me. She replied by saying "No baby he can't kill you, God is in control. God will not allow that". I talked to her until I returned back home. As soon as I got into my house I ran in my room and fell down on my knees and asked the Lord to please help me. I asked God to give me strength because I was so weak.

I couldn't wait until my children came home from school to keep me company because it was a real struggle for me to be in my house alone. I was so paranoid. When my children did come home I ran to the door to meet them. My daughter came home first. When I saw her I wanted to hug her because I was so glad to see her. She knew something was wrong so I explained to her what I was going through and that I was glad she was home.

It was the week-end and both of my children wanted to hang out with their friends. I tried to get them to stay home with me, but they begged me to let them go. I didn't want to deprive them of their fun so I told them they could go.

I decided to call an evangelist from my church that lives in Burgaw and ask her if I could come over to her house and sit with her for awhile. She told me yes so I drove to Burgaw and stayed with her for a couple of hours then drove back home.

When I got back home I realized I just couldn't stay in my house by myself, so I called the evangelist in Burgaw and asked her if I could spend the night with her. She said yes, so I packed a bag and drove back to Burgaw to spend the night with her.

As I drove to Burgaw I asked the Lord why I couldn't stay in my home. He said it was because I still had unused patches in my night table. He also told me I needed to get rid of them, clean my house and pray.

The following morning when I got ready to leave, the evangelist's porch steps had ice on them and I slid all the way down them and hurt my toe. The evangelist came running and asked me did I fall and was I alright. She heard the fall all the way from the back of the house where her bedroom was. I told her I was alright and that I knew the devil was out to get me, but he was still a liar.

When I got home I took the rest of the patches out of my night table and threw them in the garbage. Then I got dressed for church and went to church. I was determined the devil wasn't going to stop me from going to church.

When I came home from church I began cleaning my house from top to bottom. When I got finished cleaning I went before the Lord to pray. As I was praying God revealed to me the meaning of the dream I had when I was very sick. He said me pulling the yellow stuff out of my mouth meant that was him cleaning me up from all the stuff that went into my body from the patches.

By going through my ordeal with the patches I have learned to respect pastors, elders and evangelist and everyone else who is called to preach the gospel. I realize when someone is called to do a work for God the enemy will come against them full force to try to stop the work of God from being done, but I also know that even though the test or trial may seem hard at the time God is able to keep us and help us to get through them victorious if we lean and depend on him.

One week before I got ready to do my initial sermon fear and doubt tried to set in so I had to go back before the Lord and ask him to let me see myself the way he saw me and to give me the courage and boldness I needed to do his will. God is a faithful God because when I got up from talking with the Lord my heart and mind were set on doing what the Lord wanted me to do.

I did my initial sermon on March 20, 2005. While in the pastor's office I was asked was I nervous. I answered with a yes. My pastor is very funny. He said good! It was normal for me to be a little nervous.

When the pastor, the two ministers and I entered the sanctuary to take our places on the pulpit praise and worship was going on. Even though in times past I notice alot of preachers would sit and meditate while praise and worship was going on I couldn't follow their pattern because I am one who loves to praise the Lord and not doing it would make me feel out of place. I joined with them as they praised and worshiped the

Lord. By the time praise and worship was over I didn't feel nervous because of the Spirit of God that was upon me.

The devil however didn't give up. He had to try one more attack before I got ready to preach. As I sat waiting to go up to preach, the devil attacked me in my back. I felt as if someone had taken a knife and stuck it in my back and began to turn it from right to left. I broke out in a real bad sweat as I tried not to let anyone know what I was experiencing. The pastor leaned over toward me and asked me did I want a bottle of water. I told him yes. The pastor asked one of the ushers to get me a bottle of water from his office. While the usher was getting water the pain in my back was so severe I had to lean down a little as I pleaded the blood of Jesus against the enemy. I commanded the devil to take his hands off of me and immediately the pain left and I stood with Holy Ghost boldness and gave the sermon the Lord gave me to give to his people.

Three months after doing my initial sermon our church planned to attend the ordination service that was held once a year in New York City. About two weeks before it was time for our church to go to New York I realized I didn't have the money to go. I expressed to my pastor I might not be able to go because I didn't have the money. He said he really wanted me to go because he wanted me to be ordained as an evangelist.

I wanted to go but I knew I needed a sufficient amount of money to be able to go. I needed money for my hotel stay, food for the banquet and a little spending money. I really wanted to go so I prayed and asked the Lord if it was his will for me to go to supply the money for me to go.

As I was praying the Lord spoke to me and told me to ask my daughter's brother by my daughter's father for the money. God told me what to say and how much he was going to give me. God's words were and I quote "God tell Junior I told you to ask him to sew a seed and help me to go to New York to be ordained an evangelist." God said he was going to give me two hundred dollars, but God instructed me not to ask for any amount. God also said Junior's heart was prepared and because of his obedience he is going to bless him.

The following day I went to Leland, N.C. I called Robert James Jr. from my cell phone and asked him could I speak with him. Junior asked me what I wanted to speak with him about. I told him I needed to speak with him in person because I wanted to look him eyeball to eyeball. He told me he would be at his car shop at three thirty and to meet him there.

I didn't want to drive back to Wilmington and then back to Leland again, so I went to Junior's aunt's house to visit with her until it was time for me to meet Junior. When three thirty came I went to Junior's shop to meet with him.

My exact words to Junior were "God told me to ask you to sew a seed to help me to go to New York to be ordained." I explained to him I had one hundred dollars, but that wasn't nearly enough. I explained to him how many nights I would need a hotel room for and the cost of the banquet. Without hesitation Junior stood up, pulled two one hundred dollar bills from his pocket and laid them on his desk. Immediately I began leaping and praising God because Junior gave me exactly what God told me he was going to give me. After I calmed down I explained to Junior what had just happened and I told him God said because of his obedience God was going to bless him.

Junior and I sat for about a half an hour talking about the goodness of the Lord. I even told Junior I thought he was going to call me the nick name he sometimes called me jokingly when we weren't saved. Junior always called me a crook. Junior told me he knew God sent me to ask him for the money. He said he didn't mind doing what God wanted him to do because God has been so good to him already.

When I arrived home I called my daughter's friend's father to tell him what God had done for me and because his daughter wanted to go to New York and wanted me to ask her father could she go. My daughter's friend's father said he would pay for our entire hotel stay if I took his daughter with us. I was shocked! I asked him was he serious. He said yes and that God laid it on his heart to do it. I was so excited that I called my pastor and told him what God had done for me. God is so faithful. He provided more than enough for me, my daughter and my daughter's friend to go to New York, money to eat with and even money to buy a few things with from the mall. In return I needed to share my blessing with someone else, so I invited a mother and an evangelist to share our room at a very low price.

Friday night testimony service was going on when the Lord told me to stand up and give my testimony. God told me to stand up and tell the saints not to let my clothes fool them. He told me to tell them how I was on drugs and he delivered me. He told me to tell the saints that he healed my body of the HIV virus and how I was a prostitute and he saved and delivered me. At first I was reluctant because the church was very big and there were alot of people there, but the Lord kept at me to stand and say what He told me to say.

I turned to one of my sisters in the Lord and told her I thought the Lord wanted me to give my testimony. She replied by saying "Well you know what you better do!"

The congregation was singing a song and I hoped after the song was over, the praise and worship leaders would move on with the service and testimony service would be over. I wouldn't have to stand before all the people and say what the Lord wanted me to say, but when the song was over the worship leaders asked would there be another testimony. I immediately stood up and said what the Lord told me to say and before I knew it the Spirit of God moved upon several people throughout the sanctuary. Even I began rejoicing with a dance. When the Lord got finished moving, another sister stood up and testified that God had filled both of her sons with the Holy Ghost while saints were rejoicing.

I thank God I was obedient and said what he told me to say and for moving in the hearts and minds of his people. I've learned to obey God even when I don't understand because God does everything for a reason no matter how big or small I may think the task is. God is still proving himself to me each day.

While I was in New York attending the ordination service I didn't attend the banquet because God laid it on my heart not to go. Me, a sister and a minister from my home church stayed in a room on Miracle Mountain talking about the goodness of the Lord. We spent time together, encouraging one another and building a closer relationship with one another.

At the ordination service there were pastors, bishops and saints from many different countries present. They were from countries such as: Africa, India, Jamaica, Canada and Central America; Chile, Guatemala, and Haiti and that's just to name a few. There are 225 Salvation and Deliverance Churches worldwide. Salvation and Deliverance Ministry was founded by Apostle William Brown.

It was a wonderful experience being in the presence of my fellow brothers and sisters from around the world. The presence of the Lord was powerful. People were saved, set free and delivered.

I was ordained on June 19th 2005 and my life will never be the same. I thank God for his love, his kindness and his tender mercies and for choosing me to show forth his glory by taking me "FromDarkness into His Marvelous Light".

I am a living witness of what God can do! The same thing

he did for me he can do for anyone who surrenders their will and their way over to him. God loves us all and he has no special person. He came to seek and to save all who are lost: drug addicts, prostitutes, liars, thieves, murderers, whoremongers, the sexually abused, the motherless and fatherless or what ever your case may be. Jesus came, died and rose on the third day with all power in his hand, ascended up into heaven and is seated at the right hand of God, making intercession for us, that you too may have life and have it more abundantly.

All you have to do is confess with your mouth and believe in your heart that Jesus died for your sins, accept the Lord Jesus as your personal Savior and ask him to come into your heart. Be baptized in the name of our Lord and Savior Jesus Christ. Fast, pray, read your bible and ask the Lord for the gift of the Holy Ghost; find a bible believing church and agree in your heart to walk up-right before God and you too will daily experience life changing experiences.

www.ingramcontent.com/pod-product-compliance
Lightning Source LLC
LaVergne TN
LVHW050536160826
845677LV00011B/2060

* 9 7 9 8 8 9 5 6 9 9 3 4 8 *